Low-Carb Dieting

FOR

DUMMIES®

by Katherine B. Chauncey, PhD, RD

WILEY

Wiley Publishing, Inc.

Low-Carb Basics For Dummies®

Published by
Wiley Publishing, Inc.
111 River St.
Hoboken, NJ 07030-5774
www.wiley.com

Publisher's Acknowledgments

Senior Project Editor: Zoë Wykes
Technical Editor: Kathryn Kolasa, PhD, RD
Nutrition Analyst: Patty Santelli
Editorial Manager: Rev Mengle
Cartoon: Rich Tennant, www.the5thwave.com

About the Author

Katherine Chauncey, PhD, RD, is an Associate Professor in the Department of Family and Community Medicine at Texas Tech University School of Medicine. She received her BS from the University of Arkansas and her MS and PhD from Texas Tech University. She has more than 25 years of experience in the field of nutrition. Dr. Chauncey maintains a clinical nutrition practice and participates in patient care activities within the School of Medicine. Dr. Chauncey is a Fellow of the American Dietetic Association and member of the Society of Teachers of Family Medicine.

Table of Contents

The 5th Wave

By Rich Tennant

"I substitute tofu for eye of newt in all my recipes now. It has twice the protein and doesn't wriggle around the cauldron."

Chapter 1

Getting the Lowdown on Low-Carb Living

In This Chapter

▶ Understanding low-carb eating

▶ Choosing the best carbs for your body

▶ Maintaining a low-carb lifestyle

*W*elcome to *Low-Carb Basics For Dummies.* You've probably heard a lot in the media, as well as from friends
and family, about the benefits of low-carb eating. That may be
what encouraged you to pick up this book and carry it home
(after paying for it, of course!). You may have been drawn in
by the claims of staying slim and trim while eating fat-full
delicious foods, but you may not be so sure about removing
all carbohydrate foods — such as fruits and vegetables —
entirely from your diet.

Well, look no further — this could well be the eating plan for
you. Gone are the days of fruit-free diets and fatty steaks
smothered in béarnaise sauce. Read on for a low-carb eating
plan you can follow healthfully and deliciously for the rest of
your life.

First, about This Book

One of the best things about this book, or any *For Dummies* book for that matter, is the fact that you can start just about anywhere and find something that's interesting and relevant. So feel free to start wherever you want and move around at your leisure. Here's a little guidance to get you started:

✔ If you're not sure whether the plan is right for you, take a look at Chapter 3. It's full of information on discovering your own personal health history, assessing your current health situation, and specifics on why this plan can work for you.

✔ If you want tips on eating out the low-carb way, check out Chapter 8.

✔ If you never realized that supermarkets are very systematic about their floor plans, navigate your way to Chapter 7. Your shopping experience will never again be the same.

Wherever you start or end up, you'll see little icons pop up here and there throughout this book. Here's what they mean:

The Tip icon marks things that are sure to help you in your journey to lifelong good health.

The Remember icon points out important information that's reinforced throughout a section of the book. You'll do well to remember this information.

Pay particular attention to the Warning icon to steer clear of situations that could be seriously dangerous or hazardous. Exercise some extra caution.

This little graphic marks information that's interesting but not essential for you to understand. You can skip over the text if it doesn't appeal to you and still enjoy the rest of the book.

The Whole Foods icon marks info that's specific to the eating plan I've developed.

Green Light foods are free foods that you can eat anytime anywhere. They're primarily vegetables, fruits, lean meats, and low-fat cheeses.

Because my intention in this book is to provide you with the basics of a low-carb lifestyle, I give you information about the types of foods and quantities to eat, rather than specific recipes.

Mapping Out Low-Carb Eating

Eating in America has changed. Americans eat out more frequently, eat larger portions of food, and eat more foods with little resemblance to their form in nature. As a result, more Americans are struggling to find a healthy lifestyle eating plan.

Unlike many other popular low-carb eating plans available today, this plan helps you control, *but doesn't entirely eliminate,* the intake of refined sugars and flour, and it encourages you to eat whole, unprocessed food. You may be surprised to see that the plan contains moderate amounts of starch, protein, and fat. That's because the plan allows your nutritional needs to be supplied *naturally.*

I help you focus your eating on natural, unprocessed foods whenever possible, particularly fresh fruits and vegetables, lean meat and protein, and low-fat dairy. I give you guidelines for appropriate serving sizes of carbohydrates. This is not the eat-all-the-fat-and-protein-you-can-stuff-in-your-face plan. But don't fret, you'll definitely feel full and energetic.

 By improving the quality of the carbohydrates you eat, and by controlling your daily intake of starchy carbs (like breads, pasta, and starchy vegetables), you'll experience many healthy benefits including increased energy, improved mood, and better sleeping — plus, you can lose weight as well (if that's your goal).

Eating Low-Carb or Low-Fat?

Currently, the debate rages between proponents of low-fat and low-carb diets. I'm sure you've heard the sound bite, "Fat makes you fat." Most Americans have gotten the low-fat dieting message. But even so, more than half of adult Americans are overweight. Our overall percentage of calories from fat went down, primarily because the actual number of calories we eat has gone up.

We are eating more food than ever. Carbohydrates have replaced much of the fat in the American diet — and the increased food intake means an increased carbohydrate intake. This increased carbohydrate intake is largely sugars, sweeteners, and processed flour. The increase in carbohydrates from these refined sources has had a direct impact on the health (and waistlines) of Americans.

What are the basics?

If you've looked into low-carb eating plans, you've probably found more than a few that require you to banish carbs from your diet entirely. And, if you like carbs the way most people do, you've probably thrown down those books with a mixture of fear and frustration. Don't worry — the guidelines I give you in this book do *not* ask you to remove carbs from your diet completely. Instead, I want to get you thinking about the quality of the foods you consume, rather than the number of carb grams those foods contain. Rest assured that you'll be allowed enough carb grams for good health.

This lifestyle eating plan is focused on enjoying *whole* or *unprocessed foods* and enjoying the healthy side effects, including having more energy, stabilizing your blood-sugar levels, losing weight, and improving your self-confidence. (Whole foods are fruits, vegetables, grains, beans, nuts, and seeds that have not been processed to remove vitamins, minerals, fiber, and so on. They are foods that are sold to consumers in close to the same state that nature provides them.)

Most foods contain some carbohydrates. Even an 8-ounce glass of skim milk contains 12 grams of carbs. A cup of broccoli contains 8 carb grams. And yet, both milk and broccoli are packed full of other nutritional benefits, including vitamins, nutrients, fiber, and *phytochemicals* (plant chemicals). If you strictly limit the number of carb grams in your diet without considering the *quality* of the carbs you eat, you'll be missing out on some key foods that will enhance your overall good health.

On a healthful low-carb plan, you're limited to five carbohydrate servings a day, but many foods that contain carbohydrates are absolutely *free* (which means that you can have as many of them as you want, without counting them in your daily carb allowance). Here are some quick tips on which foods to focus your attention on and which to pass by:

✔ **Don't be afraid of fruit.** Fruit does contain carbohydrates, but the carbs in fruit give it a delicious *natural* sweetness, which is partnered with a ton of vitamins, fiber, and relatively few calories. Increasing your fruit intake is a great way to help you wean yourself off *refined sugars* (refined sugars are sugars like table sugar and high-fructose corn syrup that are added to processed foods). Fruits make a great dessert option and, because they come pre-portioned in their own natural package, they're a great choice for grab-and-go snacks.

✔ **Look at leafy green and non-starchy vegetables.** Leafy greens, like spinach, watercress, cabbage, and romaine lettuce, and non-starchy vegetables, like green beans, broccoli, carrots, and tomatoes, are almost limitless. You can further vary your diet by trying new preparations of old favorites and partnering them with new choices.

✔ **Remove refined sugars from your life.** Refined sugars provide calories, but lack vitamins, minerals, and fiber. The amount of refined sugar in the American diet is a disastrous, but fairly recent, development. Watch out for hidden sugars in breads, lunch meat, and salad dressings. Pay attention to the not-hidden sugars in non-diet sodas, cookies, and candy.

And, for those five carbohydrate servings you're allowed to eat each day, choose from the following:

✔ **Check out legumes.** *Legumes* (leh-GOOMS) are foods like peas, beans, and peanuts. They are nutritional powerhouses that add fiber to your diet, are naturally low in fat, are a great source of protein, and are very inexpensive. Look for several varieties at your market including canned, dried, and fresh. Legumes make great additions to salads, serve as excellent side dishes, and make healthy delicious entrees in their own right.

✔ **Choose whole grains whenever possible.** Look for *whole grains* (grains that still have their bran and nutrients intact) as the first ingredient on a food nutrition label's ingredients list (see Chapter 7). Items made from whole grains tend to be higher in fiber, lower in sugar, and have a stabilizing effect on blood sugar levels compared to their refined-grain counterparts.

✔ **Introduce more soy products into your diet.** Soy foods contain both carbs and protein, making them off-limits on many low-carb eating plans. Not so with my plan. In fact, if you're a vegetarian, you can substitute soy products for lean proteins in your diet and still get many of the nutritional benefits this plan has to offer. Regardless of whether you're a vegetarian, adding more soy to your diet can offer tremendous health benefits, including a reduced risk of several types of cancer and heart disease, as well as more-balanced hormone levels.

Whether low-carb eating is right for you

Take a good look at Chapter 3 to determine if low-carb eating is right for you. But for now, the following are *all* good reasons to follow this low-carb plan:

✔ If your personal health history includes the precursors to diabetes, high blood pressure, or heart disease

✔ If you're concerned about stabilizing your blood sugar levels

✔ If you're tired of the way convenience foods and prepackaged, sugar-laden foods make you feel

✔ If your Body Mass Index (BMI) is 30 or above (turn to Chapter 3 to determine your BMI)

Discovering Whole Foods

The most important element of the eating plan is the introduction of whole foods into your diet. A *whole food* is any food that's not refined or processed. Fresh, frozen, or canned fruits and vegetables are whole foods; French fries are not. A sirloin steak is a whole food; a breaded veal cutlet is not. Whole-grain bread is a whole food; white bread is not.

The more refined a food is, the fewer vitamins and nutrients and the less fiber the food has. If you see a food that's refined but has been fortified with vitamins and minerals, like sugary breakfast cereal, be wary. These vitamins aren't as easily used

by your body for all of its vital processes as their naturally occurring counterparts. And 99 times out of 100, the food contains more sugar than your body needs.

Living the Low-Carb Way

Low-carb eating will become second nature to you quickly. The key to your success is planning. Plan your meals and plan your shopping trips to fit with your low-carb lifestyle. You can minimize impulse buys by having a plan to stick to.

 Be aware of the layout of the stores where you shop for food. For example, stick to the perimeter of a grocery store for most whole-food choices (such as fresh produce, low-fat dairy products, and lean meats). When you enter the center aisles for dried beans, canned vegetables, or whole oats, avoid the temptation to toss prepackaged dinner helpers, chips, cookies, or sugary cereals into your cart.

With a little effort, you can navigate your way around a low-carb kitchen. My pantry tends to be full of canned whole veggies rather than canned soup, which typically contains more sodium and modified food starch than vegetables. I use fresh or frozen beef, canned beans, and tomatoes to make my own chili instead of buying premade canned chili. Find your own shortcuts to make your life easier *and* low-carb friendly.

 When dining out, don't be afraid to ask for substitutions. If your steak comes with French fries, ask for a side of veggies instead. Most restaurants, even fast-food restaurants, have a house or green salad that's a great addition to any meal and totally free on this eating plan. Just get your dressing on the side. For more tips on dining out, skip ahead to Chapter 8.

Identifying Other Factors for Overall Health

When you hear someone say, "I'm on a diet," they usually mean, "I'm trying to lose weight." But the word *diet* (coming from the Latin *dieta,* or "daily regimen") can also refer simply to the food you eat day in and day out. I want to change your daily food plan for the rest of your life. If you want to lose weight, that's okay, too. So, in this section, I talk about factors to consider when you're charting your low-carb-eating-plan progress.

Exercise and low-carb eating: Your partners in fitness

Exercise isn't just a necessary part of life, it's fun! With so many different forms of exercise available, you're sure to find one that matches your interests and lifestyle. You don't have to run out and buy Spandex, join a gym, and attend a Pilates class this week. Just pulling weeds in the garden or mowing the lawn can get your heart pumping. Find a friend to walk with you during your lunch break. Anything that gets you moving is a great addition to your lifestyle.

The effects of exercise are cumulative, which means that you don't have to get your 30 minutes a day in one shot. You can take a 15-minute walk around the block in the morning, and another 15-minute walk after dinner.

Daily exercise stabilizes your blood sugar levels, improves your cardiovascular health, increases your strength and stamina, and helps you get a better night of sleep. You may feel more tired immediately after beginning a new exercise program, but you should quickly enjoy increased energy levels, as well as an improved mood because of the *endorphins* running rampant in your bloodstream.

Endorphins are chemical signals in your blood that act like your body's own version of morphine or painkillers. Production of endorphins in the body is linked to increased exercise and produces a feeling of euphoria, sometimes labeled as *runner's high* in athletes.

The more you exercise, the more lean muscle you develop. And the more lean muscle you develop, the higher your resting *metabolism.* (Your metabolism is sort of your internal rhythm, or the rate at which you burn calories when completely at rest.) With a higher resting metabolism, you burn more calories while you're sleeping, working at your desk, or even just breathing. How's that for efficiency?

Exploring vitamins and supplements

You're encouraged to take in most of your vitamins and minerals through the whole foods that you consume. However, a few important exceptions may exist.

If you're at risk for osteoporosis, you'll want to calculate your calcium intake, and if it doesn't meet your daily need, add a calcium supplement to your daily regimen. Certain health conditions and certain stages in life may make a vitamin or mineral supplement appropriate as well. Antioxidant nutrients like vitamins C, E, and beta-carotene and the minerals zinc, copper, selenium, and manganese may help lower your risk of disease and the ravages of aging.

Maintaining Your Low-Carb Lifestyle

As with making any long-term change to your diet, the key to enjoying the ultimate benefits of your low-carb lifestyle is sticking with the plan. Chapter 6 is loaded with tips and tricks to help you set yourself up to succeed.

Making the commitment

The first step in making the low-carb commitment is mental or psychological. Customize your food habits to meet the demands of your lifestyle and your low-carb eating plan. If you can get your family, roommates, or other housemates to follow the plan with you, you'll definitely have a better shot at success by removing tempting foods and sweets from your cabinets and fridge. But don't stress if others aren't interested. You can still cook for the whole family and adjust your own portion sizes to coincide with this plan. You'll just need to be careful not to indulge in cookies or snacks.

Planning ahead

Let your lifestyle help determine your food-plan strategy. If you know that you have no time in the mornings, prepare your healthy breakfast and lunch the night before. Plan your meals before you're hungry. Making healthy choices is much more difficult when you're hungry and refined foods are handy.

The rise of prepackaged, convenience foods has increased the amount of refined sugar in the American diet, but your busy schedule doesn't have to be a barrier to healthy eating. Keep healthy snacks on hand in snack-size resealable plastic bags for easy treats. You'll eliminate the urge to grab cookies, chips, and crackers.

Cook meals in quantity. Roast a large turkey or ham for lots of leftovers and soups or salads. Double entree sizes so that you can eat one and freeze one for later. Buy reusable plastic containers that go from freezer to microwave for your own frozen lunch entrees.

Picking yourself up when you fall

I wish I could say that no one ever slips up on this plan, that no one ever gives in to temptation and succumbs to that extra baked potato or slice of cake. But the fact is that giving in to temptation is part of life. You're human and, therefore, you aren't perfect. However, don't beat up on yourself when you slip up, and more importantly, don't use it as an excuse to throw all your progress out the window. These small setbacks can be the gateway to long-term success. If you can learn from them and make better choices in the same situation next time, you can have better overall health and weight control.

Chapter 2

All Carbs Are Not Created Equal

In This Chapter

▶ Identifying the different kinds of carbohydrates

▶ Understanding the glycemic load of foods

▶ Setting realistic carbohydrate goals

*W*here is carbohydrate? It's in sugar, bread, potatoes, cereal, pasta, beans, chips, cookies, cake, soft drinks, fruit, vegetables, and dairy. It's even a substance in your blood that your body depends on for fuel. Carbohydrate is everywhere except in meats and animal fats, and most of it is pretty tasty. Carbohydrate as a nutrient source is an important part of a healthy diet. To restrict all dietary intake of carbohydrate, the way some low-carb diets prescribe, regardless of its food source is short-sighted. Dismissing fruits, vegetables, whole grains, and beans simply because they contain carbohydrates could be disastrous to your health, in both the short run and the long run.

The intake of refined carbohydrate foods (foods that have been stripped of their nutritional value during processing), yielding little nutritive value except calories, has overwhelmed our sedentary nation. Children and athletes can consume larger amounts of starches and sugars with less harm than can relatively inactive people; but many people tend to eat a greater amount of these kinds of carbohydrates than they can handle. So, before you start to lower your carbohydrate intake, you need to get a sense of the various forms and functions of carbohydrates. This will help you decide which ones to keep and which ones to control.

A sugar by any other name would probably still end in *-ose*

There are six sugars that are most important to nutrition, and they all end in the suffix *-ose*. Originally from the Greek *glykys,* meaning "sweet" and *gleukos,* meaning "sweet wine," the French used the word *glucose* to describe the first discovered simple sugar. Since that time, with each sugar discovery, scientists have continued in the tradition of giving each sugar a name ending with *-ose*. (Think glucose, fructose, galactose, maltose, lactose, and sucrose.) Bottom line: If you see a food label with a listing for something that you don't recognize, and it ends in *-ose,* odds are it's a sugar.

All dietary carbohydrates, from starch to table sugar, can be converted into glucose to be used as fuel for the body, especially the brain. How active you are governs your need for this fuel. So if you're not very active and your body's reserved carbohydrate fuel is full, you'll store the surplus as fat.

Understanding Carbohydrates

The primary role of carbohydrates in human nutrition is to supply an indispensable commodity — energy. When carbohydrates yield energy at the rate of 4 calories per gram, they spare proteins from being used for energy so that proteins can do the building and repairing of body tissues that they're uniquely suited for. Without sufficient carbohydrates, your body will burn its protein for fuel. Carbohydrates appear in virtually all plant foods and in only one food taken from animals — namely, milk.

The sugar connection

Carbohydrates come in three main sizes: sugars whose atoms are arranged in a single ring (monosaccharides); sugars made from pairs of rings (disaccharides); and long chains of single-ring carbohydrates (polysaccharides). The monosaccharides and disaccharides are known as *simple carbohydrates;* the polysaccharides are known as *complex carbohydrates*. Your body almost invariably converts carbohydrates, whatever form they come in (except dietary fibers), to its own energy source, commonly referred to as *blood sugar*.

What carbs give you beyond nutrition

Six essential nutrients are necessary for good health and for life: protein, carbohydrate, fat, vitamins, minerals, and water. Only protein, carbohydrate, and fat provide energy in the form of calories. Your body needs all of these nutrients to stay alive. Scientists are learning, however, that *other* components are essential for *good health*. These components don't yield energy either (in other words, they don't have calories), but their role in disease prevention is vital. I cover these non-nutrient components in the following sections.

Fiber

Dietary fiber is found in plant foods and is mainly the fiber component of a plant's cell walls, which aren't digested by the enzymes in your intestinal tract and, therefore, don't provide you with any energy. Dietary fiber comes in two types: soluble and insoluble.

As with anything in nutrition, you need a balance of both types of fiber. *Soluble* fiber helps to lower your LDL ("bad") cholesterol and lowers your rate of glucose absorption. *Insoluble* fiber helps to soften your stool and lowers your risk of some kinds of cancer. Each type of fiber performs a distinct function and is necessary for good health.

 Traditionally, soluble fiber got the credit for lowering cholesterol, while improvement of bowel regularity was attributed to insoluble fiber. The truth is that both fiber sources improve regularity and lower blood cholesterol.

Phytochemicals

Phytochemicals are compounds that exist naturally in all plant foods (*phyto* comes from the Greek word for "plant"). Hundreds of thousands of *phytochemicals* (or plant chemicals) are found in the foods you eat. An apple alone has over 380 kinds of phytochemicals! Carbohydrate foods such as fruits, vegetables, grains, legumes, seeds, licorice root, soy, and green tea all contain these plant chemicals. Phytochemicals are best supplied from fruits and vegetables — not from supplements.

Phytochemicals contain protective, disease-preventing compounds. More than 900 different phytochemicals have been identified as components of food, and many more phytochemicals continue to be discovered every day. Just one serving of vegetables gives you about 100 different phytochemicals!

Think of *phyto* as "fight-o." Every mouthful puts disease fighters in your body. Phytochemicals occur to protect the plant from disease and destruction and continue to protect the humans who eat the plants.

Phytochemicals are associated with the prevention and/or treatment of at least four of the leading causes of death in the United States — cancer, diabetes, cardiovascular disease, and hypertension. They are involved in many processes including those that help prevent cell damage, prevent cancer cell replication, and decrease cholesterol levels.

Here's a quick list of a few noteworthy phytochemicals and their sources in carbohydrate foods:

Phytochemical	*Sources*
Allyl sulfides	Garlic, onions, leeks, and chives
Capsaicin	Hot peppers
Carotenoids	Dark green and yellow fruits and vegetables
Coumarins	Citrus fruit, tomatoes
Ellagic acid, phenols	Grapes, berries, cherries, apples, cantaloupe, watermelon
Flavonoids	Citrus fruit, tomatoes, berries, peppers, carrots
Genistein	Beans, peas, lentils
Indoles	Broccoli, cabbage
Isoflavones	Soybeans, dried beans
Lignans	Flaxseed, barley, wheat

Phytochemical	*Sources*
Lutein, zeaxanthin	Spinach, kale, collard greens, romaine lettuce, leeks, peas
Lycopene	Tomatoes, red peppers, red grapefruit
Saponins	Soybeans, dried beans
Phytic acid	Whole grains (barley, corn, oats, rye, wheat)

Discovering How Carbs Affect Your Blood Sugar Levels

The *glycemic index* measures the effects of equal quantities of different carbohydrates on blood glucose levels. Introduced over 20 years ago, the glycemic index challenged traditional thinking about carbohydrate effects on blood sugar. Traditional theory stated that simple carbohydrates, such as orange juice, raised blood glucose levels quickly, while complex carbs, such as crackers, raised blood glucose levels more slowly. However, glycemic index values showed some simple carbohydrates to raise blood glucose slowly and some complex carbohydrates to raise blood glucose quickly.

The *glycemic load* is a measurement that is calculated from the glycemic index and is used to evaluate the glucose response in a normal serving of a particular food. The formula is the glycemic index multiplied by the number of grams of carbohydrate in a serving, divided by 100. Don't worry about the mathematical formulas right now. Just remember that you can use glycemic load to evaluate the kinds of foods in your diet. If it appears that most of your foods are on the high glycemic load level and those foods are low in nutritive factors, then exchanging some of those high glycemic choices for low glycemic choices would be a good idea. If most of your foods fall into the low glycemic category, then chances are you're eating a very healthy diet.

 You can find more information on glycemic index (GI) and glycemic load (GL), as well as an online database of the GI and GL of foods at www.glycemicindex.com. This Web site is from the University of Sydney, Australia, where considerable research is being conducted on the glycemic value of foods.

Insulin effects

Insulin follows glucose in the glycemic index response. In other words, as glucose increases, so does insulin. Insulin works to maintain your body's normal blood glucose levels. Some scientists argue that refined carbohydrates like white sugar, white rice, and processed cereals raise blood glucose rapidly, causing an outpouring of insulin. This excess insulin can drop blood glucose levels too rapidly. This sudden drop in blood glucose stimulates hunger and overeating. On the other hand, unrefined carbohydrates such as whole wheat, brown rice, bran cereals, and fruits and vegetables are digested more slowly and contain dietary fiber. These foods raise blood glucose levels slowly without overstimulating insulin, resulting in more-stable blood glucose levels and better appetite control.

Reducing the refined and processed carbohydrates in your diet and tailoring meal plans to your individual needs are safe practices that can have positive effects on your health and well-being. The challenge, as with any healthy modification, is staying motivated to adopt the regimen as a permanent lifestyle change.

Carbohydrate foods that are low in glycemic load seem to increase satiety and maintain consistent blood glucose and insulin levels. Non-starchy vegetables, fruits, legumes, and high-fiber whole-grain products tend to have a low glycemic load. These foods have a proven record of health benefits such as lower risk of heart disease and cancer and less gastro-intestinal diseases and are a component of any reasonable diet. Such slowly absorbed carbohydrates can contribute greatly to overall health, satiety, and weight loss.

Most refined and processed carbs are high in glycemic load and may result in hunger soon after their rapid digestion. Refined and processed carbs such as those found in cookies, crackers, white bread, and white rice have a high glycemic load; their easy digestion causes a rapid elevation in blood glucose and insulin levels. After a couple of hours, the blood glucose levels quickly decline, resulting in cravings for more food in some people. This phenomenon may have led to the coining of the phrase *carbohydrate addiction*.

You don't have to totally avoid high-glycemic-load foods. You can eat some high-glycemic foods in the presence of low-glycemic foods and the effect on your blood sugar won't be as great as it would be with high-glycemic foods alone. What you need to be aware of is the percentage of high-glycemic-load foods to low-glycemic-load foods. Try to include more low-glycemic-load foods than high-glycemic-load foods in your diet.

Building the Pyramids One Brick at a Time

The USDA Food Guide Pyramid has been around since 1992, and most people know what it is. Versions of the pyramid have been developed for specific age groups such as kids and the elderly, different ethnic groups, and different geographic areas, but they all use a similar organization of foods. Many other pyramids have been proposed to replace the USDA Food Guide Pyramid, such as the Mediterranean Diet Pyramid, the Asian Diet Pyramid, and the Latin American Diet Pyramid. These pyramids emphasize the foods of a particular culture and don't necessarily use the same organization of foods as the USDA Food Guide Pyramid. The Food Guide Pyramid was designed to promote a healthy diet. It includes a variety of whole-grain and fortified refined foods to meet nutrient needs. It was not designed for weight loss.

Unfortunately, even though the Food Guide Pyramid has increased nutrition knowledge, it hasn't changed eating habits of consumers. The Food Guide Pyramid emphasized moderately lowering fat in the diet and replacing it with bread, cereals, grains, fruits, and vegetables. Fat is a calorie-dense fuel. It provides 9 calories per gram, while carbohydrate and protein each give us 4 calories per gram. Current wisdom would say if you cut out something that gives 9 calories and replace it with something that gives 4 calories, you'll reduce your total calorie intake. Sounds reasonable, right? Take away high-fat foods and replace them with fruits, vegetables, and whole grains. Unfortunately, along with the reduced-fat message came fat-free cookies, cakes, chips, snacks, and desserts. Fat tastes good, so to trick our taste buds into thinking that fat-free foods tasted good, manufacturers loaded them with sugar. So, they didn't just replace a fat gram with a carbohydrate gram in an even swap; they replaced the fat with double, triple, quadruple the carbohydrate!

I favor the Low-Glycemic-Index Pyramid proposed by Dr. David S. Ludwig of Children's Hospital in Boston (see Figure 2-1). The Low-Glycemic-Index Pyramid is designed to prevent and treat obesity. A number of research studies suggest that diets designed to lower the insulin response to ingested carbohydrate (such as a low-glycemic-index diet) may improve utilization of stored energy (body fat), decrease hunger, and promote weight loss. The Low-Glycemic-Index Pyramid demonstrates that such a diet would have as its base abundant quantities of low-glycemic vegetables and fruits, moderate amounts of protein, legumes, reduced-fat dairy, and healthful fats, and an emphasis of whole grains over refined-grain products, potatoes, and concentrated sugars.

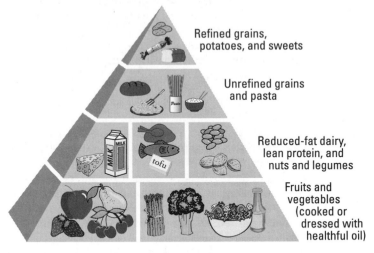

Refined grains, potatoes, and sweets

Unrefined grains and pasta

Reduced-fat dairy, lean protein, and nuts and legumes

Fruits and vegetables (cooked or dressed with healthful oil)

Courtesy of Dr. David S. Ludwig and the Journal of Nutrition

Figure 2-1: The Low-Glycemic-Index Pyramid is designed to prevent and treat obesity.

Following any eating plan that doesn't allow you to get the minimum requirements of key nutritional benchmarks, including fiber, calcium, fat, protein, and carbohydrate can have disastrous long-term health complications. Always seek input from your healthcare provider before altering your eating habits or beginning an exercise program.

Several immediate side effects can occur with a carbohydrate intake of only 20 to 30 grams. Here's a quick list of a few of the most common ones:

- **Constipation:** Severe carbohydrate restriction eliminates fruit, vegetables, and grains. The resulting low fiber intake can lead to constipation and gastrointestinal problems.

- **Dehydration and low blood pressure:** This results from the excessive water loss in the early stages of the plan.

- **Dizziness and fainting:** This can result from low blood pressure due to the dehydration. It's often felt when standing up too quickly.

- **Nausea and fatigue:** Both are often associated with *ketosis* (burning fat for fuel) and low blood-sugar levels.

- **Halitosis:** *Halitosis* is bad breath. It's also associated with an excess amount of *ketones* (a byproduct of burning fat for fuel) in your body. This occurs when someone is in *ketosis* (the process of burning fat). The odor has been described as smelling like a cross between nail polish and overripe pineapple. (Just the kind of thing you're striving for, right?)

- **Ketosis:** *Ketosis* is a condition resulting from switching from using carbs to fat as the primary energy source. As your body metabolizes fat, it gives off ketones; excess ketones show up in your urine. Although ketosis is your body's natural backup survival system, when it occurs over an extended period of time, ketosis can cause light-headedness and fogginess. In some medical conditions, prolonged ketosis can cause coma and even death. Being in ketosis continually is not normal, and the long-term safety of this condition is unknown. Ketosis is definitely not good for children.

- **Short-term weight loss:** Initial weight loss is due to water loss and levels off in about 7 to 14 weeks. Permanent weight loss occurs more slowly and only if you stay on the diet. If your purpose for low-carb eating is to lose weight, be aware that if you stop following a low-carb diet and return to normal eating, the weight usually returns.

Possible *long-term* effects of a very-low-carb lifestyle include the following:

- **Loss of muscle mass:** Your body must have a source of glucose. In diets with too low a restriction in carbohydrate (below 130 grams), your body starts to metabolize the protein in muscle tissue in order to get carbohydrate. This will eventually weaken your body.

- **Increased workload on your kidneys:** Very-low-carbohydrate diets are associated with excess protein and fat intake. High protein intake puts an added burden on the kidneys and liver. If you have diabetes, you already have an increased risk of kidney disease, so be sure to check with your physician before following a high-protein diet. If you already have kidney disease, then a low-carb diet is definitely *not* for you.

- **Kidney stones and gout:** A high protein, ketosis-inducing diet can lead to high uric acid levels in the blood, increasing the risk of kidney stones and gout.

- **Increased risk of heart disease:** Diets very low in carbohydrate are usually high in saturated fat and high in animal protein. High saturated fat increases the risk of heart disease and some forms of cancer.

- **Increased risk of some cancers:** The risk of many cancers is likely to be increased when most fruits, vegetables, whole grains, and beans are eliminated from the diet.

- **Osteoporosis:** High animal protein intake combined with the ketosis from a very low carbohydrate intake is thought to draw calcium from the bones, leading to calcium depletion and increasing the risk of osteoporosis and hip fractures. Also, rapid weight loss can accelerate bone deterioration and cause osteoporosis.

- **Vitamin and mineral deficiencies:** When entire food groups (such as fruits, vegetables, grains, and dairy) are eliminated from a diet, vitamin and mineral deficiencies can occur. High-protein, low-carbohydrate diets usually lack several vitamins and minerals such as vitamins A, C, D, the B vitamins, antioxidants that can slow the effects of aging, and calcium.

None of these complications should occur on the Whole Foods Eating Plan. On the Whole Foods Eating Plan, you're allowed five carbohydrate choices per day, because this is an amount that will allow for a healthy 1 to 2 pounds of weight loss per week. Carbohydrate from fruits and vegetables is not restricted because fruits and vegetables are so essential to good health and disease prevention.

Chapter 3

Low-Carb Eating and You!

....

In This Chapter

▶ Assessing your personal health history

▶ Looking at your own lifestyle

▶ Planning a low-carb eating strategy

▶ Snacking between meals, with low-carb treats

▶ Designing breakfast, lunch, and dinner

....

*N*ot every eating plan is beneficial to every person. Some people are in perfect health and likely also have nearly perfect diets. Others may need very strict limits or restrictions on foods due to allergies or other conditions. Still others with existing health conditions may need to cut out refined sugars but can enjoy artificially or naturally sweetened foods.

So how do you know if a low-carb diet can benefit you personally? One way is to talk with your family doctor or healthcare professional about the plan I outline in this book. But before you do, consider reading this chapter to get your low-carb ducks in a row. You'll likely be a step ahead when you actually do talk to your doctor, because your doctor will probably want you to complete some version of this assessment.

This chapter is not intended to diagnose your health problems. Its only intent is to make you aware of your risk factors. Healthy adults should have complete physical exams at least every five years beginning at age 20. Check with your family doctor to find out what's appropriate for you.

What's Your Story? Assessing Your Personal Health Risks

People metabolize carbohydrates in different ways. Some carbohydrates are beneficial to your health and others can actually be harmful to your health, depending on your own health history. Before you make a change in your diet, take a look at yourself, your family, and your lifestyle. And if you haven't seen your family doctor in a while, call and make an appointment to discuss the plan with him or her.

Knowing your BMI, blood glucose (sugar) level, total cholesterol level, HDL cholesterol, LDL cholesterol, triglycerides, and blood pressure is important. You'll probably need to take a trip to your family doctor to get much of this information, although I show you later in this chapter how to determine your BMI, and you may be able to get your blood pressure and cholesterol tested in your community. (YMCAs and even some grocery stores often offer inexpensive blood pressure and cholesterol testing from time to time, so check around.)

If you're like most people, you probably go through life not really thinking about how family history and age affect you so I'm here to tell you about a couple of things to think about:

- ✓ **Uncovering your family medical history:** What kinds of diseases or health problems are in your family? Did Grandma have diabetes? Did Uncle Joe have a heart attack in his forties? How about Mom and Dad? Are they in good health?

  The American Medical Association (AMA) can get you started with tracking your family history with their online Adult Family History Form (www.ama-assn.org/ama/pub/print/article/2380-2844.html). You can fill out the form online and then print it for your records. You can also e-mail it to family members for their input. However you gather the information, keep it up to date and share it with your physician and family.

  If you're adopted or have no contact with a biological family, start keeping a record of what you know about yourself for your current or future offspring.

✔ **Figuring out how your age affects your health:** As you age, you face increased risk of developing certain diseases. So read on to determine what role your age plays in your health.

If you get a group of 25-year-olds together, chances are you'll have a very healthy group of people. If you get that same group together 35 years later when they're 60 years old, you'll have a very diverse group in terms of their health status. As you age, you reap the benefits or destruction of your lifestyle, genetics, and exposure. We all want to live long, healthy lives. But that doesn't start at 60 — it starts when you're young. If you're older than 25, however, don't worry: A healthy lifestyle *can* start today.

Looking at your body mass index

The *body mass index* (BMI) is being used as an assessment of body size. In the past, height and weight tables developed by insurance companies classified weights by frame size (small, medium, or large), with one table for men and one for women. The body mass index looks at what people weigh and classifies their weight by degree of medical risk. The BMI is a close measurement of body fat in most people. The same table is used for men and women.

Smoking and your health

If you're a smoker, quitting smoking is the most important step you can take to improve your health. Smoking increases your risk of lung cancer, throat cancer, emphysema (a lung disease), heart disease, high blood pressure, ulcers, gum disease, and other conditions. Smoking can cause coughing, poor athletic ability, and sore throats. It can also cause face wrinkles, stained teeth, and dull skin.

Remember: It is *never* too late to quit smoking. Save your money and prolong your life — quit today. Some people fear the weight gain that sometimes comes with quitting smoking, but it's usually no more than 5 pounds and is easily remedied. Smoking is far worse than the weight gain. Your family doctor or healthcare provider can help you decide which smoking cessation method will work best for you.

Get moving: Physical activity and age

You never outgrow your need for physical activity. As you age, you need to be even more dedicated to being active. Normal aging results in a gradual decline in heart and lung function, nerve function, and muscle and bone strength. Being active improves your heart and lungs and allows you to do more work without feeling tired. Physically active older adults have faster reaction times, better balance, and better hand-eye coordination for performing manual tasks. Physical activity can reduce the number of fractures in older adults as well.

Figuring out your BMI

You can calculate your body mass index as follows:

1. **Multiply your weight (in pounds) times 703.**

2. **Multiply your height (in inches) times itself.**

3. **Take the number you get in Step 1 and divide it by the number you get in Step 2.**

   The result is your BMI.

For example, let's say you're 5 feet 8 inches tall and you weigh 175 pounds. You would multiply 175×703 to get 123,025. Then you take your height in inches (68 inches) and multiply it times itself (68×68) to get 4,624. Then $123,025 \div 4,624 = 26.6$.

A BMI of 20 to 24.9 is considered a healthy weight with no degree of medical risk. A BMI of 25 to 29.9 is considered over-weight, but not obese and has a low degree of medical risk. A BMI of 30 or greater is obesity, with a moderate to high degree of medical risk, depending on exactly how high the BMI actually is.

✔ **BMI limitations:** Because your BMI is based solely on weight and height, it may overestimate body fat in athletes and others who have a lot of muscle. If this applies to you, you'll need a measure of your body-fat percentage. (Most gyms and fitness centers have facilities and trained personnel to complete these tests.)

On the other hand, BMI may underestimate body fat in older people or others who have lost muscle. So use the

BMI as a helpful tool, but realize that its readings and scores are not absolute.

✔ **Your BMI score:** If your number is 30 or above, don't make the mistake of thinking you have to reach the 20 to 25 range before you'll see a benefit to your health. Research shows that if you reduce your weight by 10 percent or even lower your BMI number by 2 points, you'll significantly improve many health factors such as blood glucose, triglycerides, cholesterol, and blood pressure. Give yourself six months to lose 10 percent of your body weight.

If you aren't overweight or obese, but health problems run in your family, keeping your weight steady is important. Developing a regular habit of physical exercise and eating a healthy diet is the best way to prevent weight gain.

Identifying your diabetes risk

People who have diabetes have a blood glucose level (often called blood sugar level) that is too high. Everyone's blood has some glucose in it because our bodies need it for energy. But too much glucose in the blood isn't good for your health.

Diabetes comes in three main kinds:

✔ **Type 1 diabetes:** Formerly called juvenile diabetes or insulin-dependent diabetes, type 1 diabetes is usually diagnosed in children, teenagers, or young adults. In this form of diabetes, the body can no longer make insulin. Treatment for type 1 diabetes includes taking insulin shots or using an insulin pump, making wise food choices, exercising regularly, and controlling blood pressure and cholesterol.

✔ **Type 2 diabetes:** Formerly called adult-onset or non-insulin-dependent diabetes, this is the most common form of diabetes. People can develop type 2 diabetes at any age — even during childhood. In type 2 diabetes, the body either doesn't make enough insulin or the body can't properly use the insulin it does make; this condition is called *insulin resistance*. Being overweight increases your chances of developing type 2 diabetes. Treatment includes using diabetes medications and sometimes insulin, making wise food choices, exercising regularly, and controlling blood pressure and cholesterol.

✔ **Gestational diabetes:** Some women develop gestational diabetes in the late stages of pregnancy. This form of diabetes usually goes away after the baby is born. However, a woman who has had gestational diabetes has a greater chance of developing type 2 diabetes later in life.

Of the more than 17 million Americans with diabetes, most of them have type 2 diabetes, the most common form of the disease. It is estimated that nearly one-third of these people are not even aware they have the disease. One reason is that for a long time, there may not be any warning signs or symptoms. Sometimes the diagnosis may be made only after a serious complication occurs.

Type 2 diabetes is an inherited disease. If you have several family members with the disease, you should be checked for the disease regularly by your physician.

Even though there are different types of diabetes, the signs and symptoms are the same:

✔ Extreme thirst

✔ Frequent urination

✔ Extreme hunger or unusual tiredness

✔ Unexplained weight loss

✔ Frequent irritability

✔ Blurry vision

✔ Cuts or sores that heal slowly

✔ Unexplained loss of feeling or tingling in your feet or hands

✔ Frequent skin, gum, or bladder infections

✔ Frequent yeast infections

If you have one sign or symptom, that doesn't mean you have diabetes. But you should start to be concerned if you have several symptoms. A checkup with your doctor now could start you on treatment to help prevent or reduce the heart, eye, kidney, nerve, and other serious complications diabetes can cause.

Understanding lipids

Lipid is another name for fat, so blood lipids are fats in your blood. Your doctor can create a *profile* (a breakdown of the different types of fat in your blood) of your lipids to help determine the type of heart disease you are at risk for (if any) and also to help determine the dietary approach to best lower your lipids. When your doctor or healthcare provider checks your lipids, you're likely to get a list of numbers in each of the following categories:

- **Total cholesterol:** A measurement of your total blood fats, including the sum of the HDL, LDL, and VLDL cholesterol components.

- **High-density lipoprotein (HDL) cholesterol:** Commonly called "good" cholesterol because it carries excess cholesterol back to the liver, which processes and excretes the cholesterol. You want this number to be *greater* than 40 mg/dl.

- **Low-density lipoprotein (LDL) cholesterol:** Commonly called "bad" cholesterol because high levels are linked to increased risk for heart disease. Ideally, you want this number to be *below* 100 mg/dl.

- **Very-low-density lipoprotein (VLDL) cholesterol:** Determined by dividing the triglyceride number by 5. VLDL cholesterol can be converted to LDL or "bad" cholesterol.

- **Triglycerides:** Triglycerides are a blood fat that is not only affected by the fat in your diet but is increased by excess calories and excess carbohydrate in the diet. It's normal for triglycerides to increase after eating a meal, but they usually fall back to normal in two to three hours. Chronically high triglycerides have recently been linked to heart disease. You want this number to be *below* 150 mg/dl.

Spotting early problems with blood pressure

Blood-pressure readings are expressed in two numbers that reflect the pressure on artery walls when the heart contracts.

Turn to Table 3-1 for information on what your blood pressure reading means.

Federal health officials recently announced a new category for blood pressure called *prehypertension*. If the top (or systolic) number in your blood pressure reading is between 120 and 139 or if the bottom (or diastolic) number is between 80 and 89, you have prehypertension. Prehypertension is a blood pressure that doesn't require treatment with medication but still can increase your risk of heart disease and stroke. The new guidelines encourage you to make lifestyle changes such as losing weight, exercising, quitting smoking, or reducing alcohol intake.

Table 3-1   Understanding Your Blood Pressure Reading

Blood Pressure Classification	Systolic (Top Number)	Diastolic (Bottom Number)
Normal	Less than 120	Less than 80
Prehypertension	120 to 139	80 to 89
Stage 1 Hypertension	140 to 159	90 to 99
Stage 2 Hypertension	160 or greater	100 or greater

Source: National Heart, Lung, and Blood Institute (NHLBI)

Examining Your Current Lifestyle: Be Honest!

The good news here is that, unlike your age and your family history, you can make changes to your lifestyle. Some of the risk factors you can change include the foods you eat, the amount of physical activity you get, whether you smoke, and the alcohol you consume. If you have family tendencies for diabetes, heart disease, cancer, high blood pressure, and obesity, or if you're starting to show early signs of the conditions yourself, your diet and lifestyle can make those conditions better or worse.

Paying attention to what you eat

An important factor in determining whether a low-carb eating plan is right for you is your willingness to look at your current eating habits.

✔ **Record it:** Start keeping a record of everything you eat. Buy a little notebook and keep it handy so that you can write down what you eat as soon as you eat. Do this for a week — and be honest (you're only cheating yourself if you aren't). Eat as you normally would. Don't make any changes while keeping the record. If you aren't up to keeping a one-week record, then keep it for a day or two.

No matter how you do it, develop a picture of your eating pattern. Interestingly, even with all the variety in our food supply, most people eat the same seven to ten meals on a regular basis. So, what does your dietary pattern look like?

✔ **Evaluate it:** After you have a record of what you've eaten, you need to evaluate how healthy it is. To determine the number of servings you consumed, you'll need to estimate portion sizes. You'll be surprised to see that normal portion sizes are a lot smaller than you think. Here are some examples:

Portion	*Approximate size*
½ cup	About that of a woman's tight fist, or a tennis or billiard ball
1 medium fruit	About that of a man's tight fist
1 medium potato	About that of a computer mouse
1 ounce cheese	About the size of your thumb
3 ounces meat	About that of a woman's palm or a deck of cards
1 cup	A standard 8-ounce measuring cup

To assess the foods you eat, follow these steps:

1. **Look for the basic foods essential to a healthy diet, such as vegetables, whole-grain breads or cereals, lean meats, poultry, or fish, and water or other non-sweetened beverages.**

Calculate your average daily intake by taking your totals and dividing them by the number of days you kept your food record. For example, if you tallied seven fruits over a four-day period, you consumed an average of 1.75 pieces of fruit each day (7 ÷ 4 = 1.75).

2. **Look for extra foods that contribute calories but no significant nutrients, such as chips, cookies, cakes, pies, ice cream, soft drinks, fast-food meals, fried foods, pizza, biscuits, and gravy.**

   There are no recommended servings in this category so you just need to record your daily intake.

3. **Answer the following questions about your food intake:**

   - Did your intake of the foods in Step 2 equal or exceed your intake of the foods in Step 1?

   - Can you replace some of your Step 2 choices with Step 1 choices?

   - Are you starting to get the picture of your food habits?

   Step 2 food choices are okay if you're meeting your intake of the basic food groups and if your weight is in the normal range. If you're physically active, you can handle more Step 2 foods than people who aren't very active.

 The United States Department of Agriculture's Center for Nutrition Policy and Promotion has an online dietary assessment tool called the Healthy Eating Index (http://147.208. 9.33). After entering your food intake for one day (24 hours), you'll receive a nutrition analysis including the number of calories you've eaten. You'll also receive a score, rating the quality of your food choices.

Determining your level of activity

Look at the following categories of activity and mark the one that comes closest to describing how you spend your week. Unless you're in the active or very active category, plan to up your exercise by one level.

✔ **Sedentary:** Watching television, driving a car, sitting at work, playing board games, sewing, reading, writing, talking on the phone. No program of regular exercise.

✔ **Light exercise:** Ironing, dusting, doing laundry, loading/unloading the dishwasher, preparing and cooking food, walking 2 miles per hour for 10 to 20 minutes 3 to 5 times per week.

✔ **Moderate exercise:** Dancing, gardening, doing carpentry work, mopping/scrubbing, bicycling, jogging or walking at 3 miles per hour for 20 to 40 minutes 3 to 5 times per week.

✔ **Active:** Heavy work, aerobics, tennis, skating, skiing, racquetball, brisk walking at 4 miles per hour for 30 to 60 minutes 3 to 5 times per week.

✔ **Very active:** Bicycling 15 miles per hour, running 6 miles per hour, swimming, or participating in martial arts, for 45 to 60 minutes 3 to 5 times per week.

Discovering the effects of stress

Stress is unavoidable, but it can be good or bad. Normal transitions in life like getting married or having a baby bring about stress. An unpleasant coworker or difficult job situation also brings about stress. Significant stress events like the death of a spouse or child never fully go away. Stress is part of living.

How you deal with the stress is what's important. Some people respond to stress by eating poorly, being physically inactive, smoking, or drinking alcohol. Eating and bingeing just compound the stress. The temporary comfort provided by the food is followed by guilt for overeating. When stress comes, step back, take a deep breathe, and go for a walk. Buy yourself some time to relax and decompress.

Can Low-Carb Eating Help?

A low-carb diet, especially one like the Whole Foods Eating Plan (see Chapter 4), can help the following conditions:

✔ Overweight (BMI of 25 to 29.9) and obesity (BMI of 30 or greater)

✔ Type 2 diabetes and insulin resistance

✔ Heart disease

✔ High triglycerides and low HDL cholesterol

✔ High blood pressure (but only if the low-carb plan allows fruits, vegetables, low-fat dairy, whole grains, nuts, and seeds)

✔ Polycystic ovarian syndrome (PCOS), a disease in women associated with insulin resistance

If you suffer from any of the preceding conditions, going the healthy low-carb route may be exactly what your body needs. However, if you have kidney problems, you may want to find another eating plan.

As with any eating plan, be sure to consult your doctor or registered dietitian to determine if this plan is safe for you to follow given your specific health situation.

So, You Wanna Give Low-Carb Eating a Try

One key ingredient in the recipe for low-carb eating is planning. The better prepared you are to handle the unexpected obstacles that your busy life throws your way, the more successful you'll be and the sooner you'll achieve your desired results — higher energy, better sleep, lost weight, and so on.

Failing to plan is planning to fail

Should you plan your eating? Most certainly, at least until choosing healthy foods becomes automatic. You plan other important aspects of your life. Just as you plan other important events in your life, plan your eating. Why plan? To ensure success.

Developing your food-plan strategy

If you know that you have ballet lessons, soccer practice, or Cub Scouts on a particular night of the week, you can plan meals ahead of time rather than visit your local fast-food restaurant. If you know you'll be working late this week, make dinner ahead of time and freeze it for a healthy reheated meal. And you might consider just keeping a few things handy and ready in the freezer for those unexpected busy nights. Your strategy is as unique as your lifestyle.

Regardless of your lifestyle, these tips are helpful. Pick and choose your favorites.

- ✔ **Go grocery shopping only once a week.** Doing so saves you time and encourages you to at least roughly plan your daily menus instead of just grabbing whatever's handy.

- ✔ **Cook in quantity.** Instead of one entree, make two. Enjoy one right away and freeze the other one to use later.

- ✔ **Prepare larger cuts of meat like a roast, whole chicken, or a turkey breast.** It's a great way to provide several family meals but cook only once.

- ✔ **Have a marathon cooking session during the weekend.** If you're chopping onions for soup, keep chopping for spaghetti sauce. And since you're cooking in volume, you can definitely justify the cleanup of time-saving equipment like food processors. Cook and freeze for the week.

- ✔ **Write it down!** Keep a food journal, especially keeping track of your carb choices. You can review it at the end of every day to make sure that you're getting enough whole grains and legumes *and* not exceeding your daily carbohydrate choices.

Work on your own food strategy and spend some time with the Whole Foods Eating Plan:

- ✔ **Review the Green Light Foods in Chapter 4.** Mark the ones you really like and the ones you're willing to try. Add a new food to your grocery list every week.

✔ **Check out the Yellow Light list of starchy carbs, in Chapter 5.** Select the ones to use and get to know the appropriate portion sizes.

✔ **Stock up on skim milk instead of whole milk and 2 percent.**

✔ **Start replacing saturated fats with unsaturated fats.** Switch to soft tub margarine rather than butter or stick margarine. Replace full-fat cheeses with crunchy nuts in your salads.

✔ **Keep lean meats on hand for quick entrees and snacks.**

Getting Organized

Any plan is only as good as its execution, and executing your plan is much easier if you're organized and ready. Here are a few easy tips that will get you ready to go in no time.

✔ **Arrange your pantry and freezer with foods sorted by their Whole Foods Eating Plan color, like Green Light on one shelf, Yellow Light on another, and so on.** This strategy makes it easy to grab ingredients that fit your needs. You can also take a quick visual inventory of what you have and don't have on grocery-shopping day.

✔ **Stock your pantry, refrigerator, and freezer with easy-to-fix, low-carb-friendly foods, such as canned and frozen vegetables, lean meats, fish fillets, and chicken.**

✔ **Enlist members of your family to help with the planning.** Make the planning process a game. Spread a few low-carb-friendly recipes out on the table, face down. Take turns picking up recipe cards to create the weekly menu. Post the menu where everyone can see it. That way, whoever is home first knows what's for dinner and can start cooking.

✔ **Make friends with your microwave.** Microwave ovens are great for vegetables. They usually save time, retain nutrients, and maximize the natural flavor of vegetables. Microwaving is also great for heating leftover vegetables. Try microwave or quick stovetop versions of dishes you usually bake.

Always pay attention to standing times in microwave recipes. Because microwave ovens can heat unevenly, these standing times give your dish a chance to even out temperature-wise.

✔ **Use other labor-saving devices, such as a food processor, convection oven, pressure cooker, slow cooker, or indoor grill.**

Maintaining grocery lists

Keep a running shopping list so that you can jot down needed items as you think of them. Post your list in a conspicuous place, like on the fridge, and keep a pencil handy. Invite all family members to add to the list letting them know there may be substitutions for high-calorie, high-carbohydrate foods.

Take your grocery list to the store on your weekly visit. All your hard work and planning is out the window if your list stays stuck to the fridge.

Creating a snack list

Snacks are a necessary (and delicious!) part of a healthy, low-carb eating plan. Gone are the days of the nutrition advice, "Three square meals a day, and no between-meal snacks." Instead, I recommend *preventive eating,* meaning eating healthy foods before you're hungry, to stave off hunger and eliminate the urge to overeat high-carb, prepackaged snacks.

Use your Green Light foods to strategically place snacks in your day to help control your appetite at meals. Strategic times are mid-morning, mid-afternoon, before dinner, or at bedtime. Other critical times include before a party or restaurant meal when you know you'll be tempted by high-calorie foods.

Be sure to include room in your weekly menu and grocery list for preplanned snacks. Here are a few suggestions:

✔ An orange, a bunch of grapes, a big green (or red) apple

✔ An 8-ounce container of low-fat yogurt; a glass of skim, ½-percent, or 1-percent milk; skim-milk mozzarella string cheese

- ✔ A can of unsweetened applesauce, diced peaches, or mixed fruit

- ✔ Dried apricots or a handful of raisins

- ✔ Raw vegetables (baby carrots, cherry tomatoes, green beans, pepper strips, radishes, celery, cucumber) with a low-fat salad dressing

- ✔ Sliced turkey rolled up in a lettuce leaf

- ✔ Boiled shrimp with zesty cocktail sauce

Keep a chalkboard in the kitchen listing the snacks you have on hand. When you run out of one snack, just erase it or replace it with another.

Breakfast Quick and Easy

Breakfast is a meal that is often neglected and surrounded with excuses. Like, "I don't like bacon and eggs, and cereal makes me gag in the morning!" "I'm way too rushed in the morning, so I don't have enough time to eat," "I'm really not hungry when I first wake up," or, "I'm trying to lose weight, so I'll just save those calories."

None of those excuses are valid. The word *breakfast* comes from the phrase "break the fast." Our time of sleep is not only a time for rest and restoration, it's also the longest time most of us go in a 24-hour period without eating. The overnight fast from dinner until you wake up depletes the glucose stores necessary to keep your brain alert. A well-balanced morning meal ignites your mind and muscles for the day. Research demonstrates that skipping breakfast lowers mental perform-ance especially in youth and young adults.

But analyze those excuses for a minute:

- ✔ **"I don't like traditional breakfast foods."** Who says breakfast has to be bacon and eggs, cereal and milk, or pancakes and syrup? Even left-over veggie or cheese pizza, or a peanut butter sandwich with orange juice can make a good breakfast. Just about any food can be a breakfast food, except breakfasts high in refined carbo-hydrates or sugars. Sugary cereals, doughnuts, pastries, or pancakes and syrup may provide an immediate energy boost, but later in the morning you're more likely to be hungry and sleepy.

Breakfast is a good time to use one or two of your less sweet and high-fiber carb choices. Carbohydrates are necessary to provide energy. Be sure to add a lean protein or a low-fat dairy food with it to provide additional energy and to keep you feeling "full." Fiber-rich whole-grain foods can also add to the feeling of fullness.

✔ **"My mornings are too hectic. There's just not enough time."** Plan ahead and stock the fridge with grab-and-go breakfasts. Whether you eat your breakfast in your kitchen, take it with you, or keep breakfast on hand at the office, it's faster than the drive-thru and a lot healthier.

✔ **"I'm not hungry in the morning."** An early work schedule or just concentrating on getting ready for the day makes it difficult for some people to get in the mood to eat breakfast. But inevitably, hunger appears later in the morning so before you leave the house, try starting off with something small like cheese and crackers or cottage cheese and fruit. At least drink some milk or juice before heading out. Then later in the morning, eat something more substantial like a whole-wheat muffin and a handful of grapes.

Breakfast can energize you, maximize your mental potential, and keep your dietary intake on track. Start today developing your personal breakfast strategy.

Making Power Lunches

Lunch is the midday break for refueling, relaxing, and refreshing. Wherever you are — at home, the office, school, or a restaurant — take time to sit down and enjoy the food you're eating. Take a breather from whatever occupied the morning and restore your mental and physical energies for the afternoon's activities. Avoid heavy, high-carb meals. They will only leave you lethargic and sleepy at that after-lunch conference.

Use your lunchtime as a pit stop to power-up with Green Light foods and carbs low in glycemic load. For more on Green Light foods, see Chapter 4.

Because lunchtime is a time to refuel for the day, it's another good place to use one or two of your carbohydrate choices. As always, count your carb choices appropriately and if you find yourself still a bit hungrier, choose a food from the Green Light list.

 Start viewing taking your lunch as a positive thing! It keeps you from standing in the fast-food line (or sitting in the drive-thru), eating out of the vending machine (at astronomical prices), or going out for a heavier lunch than you planned. It also gives you complete control over portion sizes. Be creative when making that sandwich, and vary the menu by taking a salad or leftover foods from home. Choose foods ahead of time that fit your individual meal plan.

Satisfying Suppers

Unless your family has the luxury of similar departing times in the morning, dinner is probably the only meal at which every member is present and accounted for. Dinner deserves careful planning to ensure the right foods, but also to ensure pleasure and enjoyment. It's worth the extra effort because healthful food and pleasant feelings create a warm family atmosphere.

This is the winding down of your day and not the time to fuel up as breakfast and lunch are. Here you should be catching up on lean meats and green veggies. Keep your carb choices low at this time of day because you won't be burning them. Concentrate on building your meals around lean protein, fruit, and veggies.

Chapter 4

Loving the Whole Foods Eating Plan

*A*bout five years ago, I began to take a look at the fad diets that people found so appealing. Simplicity and the quick weight-loss results they promised were very attractive. But restrictive food choices and the inability to sustain the weight loss round out the fad-diet story. I saw people who were overwhelmed by the modern diet of super-sized fast foods, soft drinks, and salty and fat-free snacks — and their health was suffering. I also saw them struggling to lose weight by following a fad diet.

A friend gave me a fad diet for my collection that had one particularly appealing feature: It allowed you to eat as much as you wanted of certain fruits and vegetables. Other aspects of the diet weren't healthy — like allowing free intake of high-fat meats and dairy items, including bacon, sausage, butter, and whole milk — but I was intrigued by the idea of "free" foods.

Knowing how far the American diet had drifted from the basics of good health, allowing convenient refined and processed foods to replace simple, nutritional food, I used the free-food idea to develop a plan that would turn people back to basic *whole foods* (foods with little processing). Essentially, I let the foods I wanted people to eat become *free foods*. The participants could eat as many of the free foods as they wanted, whenever they wanted, without restrictions. The results of the experiment were encouraging. People not only lost weight but told me how easy following the plan was. They were eating a lot healthier, and they didn't feel deprived!

I originally designed the Whole Foods Eating Plan for weight loss in our clinics at Texas Tech. However, with medical supervision, I've used the plan to benefit people with diabetes, high triglycerides, high blood pressure, and related health problems. The plan helps you control, but doesn't entirely eliminate, the intake of refined sugars and flour, and it encourages you to eat whole, unprocessed foods. You may be surprised to see that the plan contains moderate amounts of starch, protein, and fat. That's because the plan allows your nutrition needs to be supplied *naturally* with healthy foods.

In this chapter, I show you the fruits, vegetables, and lean protein that are yours for the taking as free foods. (You can eat free foods in unlimited quantities — they're free because you don't pay for them by counting calories or using food-group choices like you might on a weight-loss plan.) This "food freeway" is the first leg of your journey to your destination of the Whole Foods Eating Plan. The plan is not a quick fix for getting rid of some extra pounds; it's a journey that can steer you back to healthy eating without forcing you to think much about quantities. But don't worry — on this trip, you'll also drop some excess baggage (in the form of unwanted pounds) along the way.

Even if you decide that the Whole Foods Eating Plan isn't for you, you can likely benefit from the information in this chapter and create your own low-carb plan. Removing processed foods, or at least reducing the amount of processed foods, from your diet is a fantastic change to just about anyone's eating plan. Just knowing which foods are the healthiest for you can help shape your eating in a healthier direction for the rest of your life.

Green-Light Foods: Foods You Can Eat without Thinking Twice

The Whole Foods Eating Plan is paved with fruits, vegetables, and protein foods, such as lean meat, fish, poultry, and low-fat cheeses. I don't want you to be hungry on this eating plan. Instead, I want you to satisfy your hunger with fruits, vegetables, and lean protein foods. I mark each list of free foods in this chapter with a Green Light icon, which means "Go ahead and make your choice."

Green Light foods are the heart and soul of this low-carb lifestyle. You don't have to weigh or measure Green Light foods — you can eat as much as you want whenever you want. Understanding portion sizes is important, of course, and I discuss portions in Chapter 5. But in this chapter, I help you replace the highly refined carbohydrates in your diet with Green Light foods.

Exploring the Free Carbs: Fruits and Vegetables

Fruits and vegetables are as good as it gets, so don't hold back! You can eat and drink as much of the carbohydrates listed in this section as you need to satisfy your hunger. The fruits and vegetables in this group do contain carbohydrates, but they're low on *glycemic load,* which ranks foods according to how they affect your blood-sugar level. The fruits and vegetables on this list are whole foods, packed with nutrients!

The glycemic load of foods shows how rapidly a food is digested, thus driving up the blood sugar. Insulin, which lowers your blood sugar, is also stimulated. Foods with a high glycemic load cause a spike in your blood-sugar level, and then insulin quickly lowers it. This sudden change in your blood-sugar level can actually *cause* hunger. (Imagine, you could be even hungrier after you eat these foods than you were before!) Foods with a low glycemic load cause a gradual, moderate increase in blood sugar without overstimulating insulin and are more satisfying to your appetite. Refer to Chapter 2 for more details on the glycemic load.

Eat and be merry with as many of the carbohydrates listed in the following sections as you need to satisfy your hunger. And remember, *free* really does mean free. You don't have to weigh or measure these foods.

To make eating fruits and vegetables more convenient, I suggest these strategies:

- ✔ **Select fruits and vegetables that require little peeling and chopping.** Good options include baby carrots, cherry tomatoes, asparagus, grapes, apples, and broccoli spears.

- ✔ **Shop the supermarket salad bars.** They offer many favorite raw vegetables and fresh fruits already cleaned and sliced.

- ✔ **Put fruits that don't need refrigeration where you can see them.** Make a habit of grabbing a few pieces on your way out the door.

- ✔ **Shop seasonal specials for better prices.**

Making fruit choices — fresh is best

Fruit is the original fast food. Nature has nicely packaged it for easy take-out. When possible, choose fresh, whole, naturally ripe fruit. But if fresh isn't available, you can buy frozen fruit year-round. If you use canned, choose fruit in 100-percent fruit juice instead of sugary syrup. If you have to buy canned fruit in a light syrup, drain it before eating. In most cases, frozen and canned fruits are just as nutritious as fresh. Besides, eating canned and frozen fruits is better than eating no fruit at all!

Bananas are not on the Green Light food list. It's not that I don't want you to eat bananas — you can find them in Chapter 5 on a Yellow Light list signaling caution. Bananas are a very good food and the number-one fruit sold in the United States. However, they're starchier than other fruits, so I count them like bread.

Here's a list of the Green Light, or free, fruits. So, go, go, go, and eat them up!

✔ **Apples, dried:** Dried apples make a great snack food and are easy to transport.

✔ **Apples, fresh:** It makes no difference what variety of apple you choose. My favorite is Golden Delicious.

✔ **Applesauce, unsweetened:** Applesauce isn't just for kids! Grownups love this tart sauce, too.

✔ **Apricots, dried:** Dried apricots make a nice snack — the dense, sweet-tart apricot taste can be quite addictive.

✔ **Apricots, fresh:** Apricots are a smooth, sweet summer fruit chock-full of nutritional goodness.

✔ **Blackberries:** Blackberries are as big as your thumb, purple and black and thick with juice.

✔ **Blueberries:** Blueberries are late-summer berries with a very rich taste. They're great sprinkled in a salad!

✔ **Cantaloupe:** Cantaloupe comes with its own bowl — just cut it in half and scoop out each half with a spoon.

✔ **Cherries, sweet, canned:** When you buy canned cherries, you're getting two for the price of one — the fruit and the canned juice.

✔ **Cherries, sweet, fresh:** Go for fresh cherries when possible, and use frozen ones in a pinch.

✔ **Dates:** A few dates are all you need to fill up.

✔ **Figs, dried:** Dried figs are readily available year-round. The easiest way to chop them is to snip them with scissors.

✔ **Figs, fresh:** Fresh figs are a healthy fruit that can satisfy a craving for sweetness.

✔ **Grapefruit:** America's wake-up fruit, this eye-opener may be rosy-fleshed or white.

✔ **Grapefruit sections, canned:** Keep canned grapefruit in the pantry, always ready to go.

✔ **Grapes:** Good nutrition comes in small packages.

✔ **Honeydew melons:** "Honey, dew try this!" (I couldn't resist.)

✓ **Kiwis:** Don't let the hairy green skin turn you off this exotic little gem — just don't forget to peel it! One kiwi has more vitamin C than ½ cup of orange juice.

✓ **Lemons:** You can use lemon to add flavor to any beverage. Lemons are great to keep in the fridge for salad dressings, as a quick flavor for fish, or to give the flavors of your other fruits a twist.

✓ **Limes:** Limes are highly underrated in the United States. I use lime to flavor everything from water and diet sodas to anything with cilantro, including salsa.

✓ **Mandarin oranges, canned:** Mandarin oranges are Chinese oranges that are very sweet! Drain them well and add to any dish.

✓ **Mangos:** Mango is delicious by itself or paired with other tropical fruits, like papaya.

✓ **Nectarines:** Nectarines are a smooth-skinned variety of peach. They taste best at the height of the season (in late June and July).

✓ **Oranges:** Oranges are a fall and winter fruit. When eaten raw, none of the precious vitamin C is lost.

✓ **Papaya:** You can bake unripe papayas like squash. They contain *papain,* the predominant ingredient in meat tenderizer.

✓ **Peaches, canned:** Canned peaches make a quick dessert for any meal. Always buy in juice, not in syrup.

✓ **Peaches, fresh:** Don't let a little peach fuzz keep you away. Peaches are delicious and loaded with nutrients.

✓ **Pears, canned:** Cut up canned pears and add them to a salad. Always buy in juice, not in syrup.

✓ **Pears, fresh:** You can purchase pears green and they will continue to ripen. They *do* get sweeter as they ripen!

✓ **Pineapple, canned:** Always buy canned pineapple in its own juice instead of syrup.

✓ **Pineapple, fresh:** Known as a symbol of hospitality in the South, fresh pineapple makes a sweet dessert.

✓ **Plums, canned:** Canned plums are a readily available treat.

✔ **Plums, fresh:** Plums come from trees found in every continent in the world except Antarctica.

✔ **Prunes, dried:** Prunes are dried, small, purplish-black, freestone plums. They're very rich in flavor.

✔ **Raisins:** Raisins are just dried grapes. They make a handy snack.

✔ **Raspberries:** When fully ripe, raspberries' caps detach. Midsummer is their prime season.

✔ **Strawberries:** Strawberries are a super food chock-full of health-giving nutrients.

✔ **Tangerines:** Tangerines are small, sweet, Chinese oranges. They peel so easily it's as if they have a zipper.

✔ **Watermelon:** Watermelon is a summertime treat that can't be beat! Try freezing watermelon juice in ice-cube trays and adding the cubes to drinks.

Go easy on fruit juices! Don't let all your fruit servings come from juice. Try to eat at least one piece of whole fruit every day.

To increase your fruit intake, try these suggestions:

✔ Nibble on grapes or raisins.

✔ Blend fresh fruit with your morning yogurt. Add a splash of orange juice and crushed ice for a homemade smoothie.

✔ Add strawberries or blueberries to your green salad.

✔ Try frozen bing cherries for an instant treat.

✔ Make your own sorbet or granita with sweet, fresh berries.

Eating your veggies, the nutrition superstars

Vegetables are nutrition superstars! They're low in calories and fat, cholesterol-free, and high in vitamins, minerals, cancer fighters, and heart protection. Veggies are nature's defense mechanism, protecting you against disease — and in the American diet, they're neglected.

Juices, juices everywhere, but how many drops (or ounces) to drink?

Choose real fruit juice, not fruit drink. Fruit drink is only 10 percent real fruit juice or less — the rest is sugar water! Drink fruit juice instead of sodas or coffee in the car. You can keep 8- to 12-ounce bottles in your refrigerator chilled and ready to go! Or you can buy them at gas stations and fast-food chains. If you need a big gulp, combine a 6-ounce juice with a 12-ounce can of *diet* lemon-lime or ginger ale soda.

Give these healthy juices a try:

✔ **Apple juice/cider:** Apple juice beats a can of soda any time and doesn't take as much to satisfy your hunger.

✔ **Cranberry juice cocktail, reduced-calorie, light:** Cranberries lessen bladder infections by preventing bacteria from clinging to the inside of the bladder and urinary tract. To avoid too much sugar, always buy the light version of cranberry juice.

✔ **Fruit juice blends, 100-percent juice:** Fruit-juice blends are a delicious drink of pure juice.

✔ **Grape juice:** Grape juice is healthy for the heart.

✔ **Grapefruit juice:** Grapefruit juice makes a great snack between meals.

✔ **Orange juice:** Make it fresh whenever possible. It's worth the extra effort.

✔ **Pineapple juice:** You can use pineapple juice to sweeten less-sweet fruits.

✔ **Prune juice:** This will improve your bowel regularity. Don't be afraid to try it.

Eat these vegetables cooked, raw, canned, frozen, micro-waved, steamed, or stir-fried **(but not deep-fried, breaded, or creamed),** with no limits on amounts:

✔ **Artichokes:** I don't recommend eating artichokes raw — not even in Texas.

✔ **Artichoke hearts:** Artichoke hearts make delicious salad material.

✔ **Asparagus:** Asparagus is a special, delicious vegetable, once only available to kings.

✔ **Bean sprouts:** Bean sprouts are the basis of a good stir-fry.

✔ **Beans (green, wax, Italian):** Beans are a go-with-anything vegetable.

✔ **Beets:** Plain or pickled, you can use the tops of beets as greens.

✔ **Broccoli:** Broccoli is America's favorite vegetable — despite what the first President Bush thinks.

✔ **Brussels sprouts:** This tiny, green, cabbage-like vegetable is a big defender of good health.

✔ **Cabbage:** Cabbage is a big cousin to the Brussels sprout. It packs a wallop against cancer and is a nutrition powerhouse.

✔ **Carrots:** It's true — carrots are good for your eyes.

✔ **Cauliflower:** The "flower of the cabbage" is a nutritious bouquet.

✔ **Celery:** Often seen on the relish tray, you can combine celery with anything.

✔ **Cucumbers:** The cucumbers you find in the supermarket are often waxed, which means you have to peel them before eating. If the skin is not waxed, however, it's edible.

✔ **Eggplant:** A purple powerhouse of prevention, eggplant should always be eaten cooked.

✔ **Green onions or scallions:** Green onions are sweetest when the bulbs are thinnest.

✔ **Greens (collard, kale, mustard, turnip):** Greens are versatile vegetables of many virtues. Vary the way you serve greens, just to shake things up.

✔ **Kohlrabi:** The knobs of kohlrabi are thickened stems. The flavor is superb, but unless the plant is young, it's frequently too fibrous in texture to be worth preparing.

✔ **Leeks:** A cousin to the onion, leeks are good heart medicine and may help prevent cancer. Be sure to soak and wash leeks thoroughly in order to remove dirt and sand deep down in the bulb.

✔ **Mushrooms:** Unless you're a mushroom expert, buy your mushrooms in a market. Those nice-looking mushrooms that pop up in your yard after a rain can be deadly.

✔ **Okra:** When included in stews, okra's gluey sap helps thicken the sauce.

✔ **Onions:** The old-time cough medicine of onion juice and honey was nothing to sneeze at. The substance in onions that makes you cry also breaks up mucous congestion.

✔ **Pepper (all varieties):** Sweet or hot, peppers are full of zesty nutrition.

✔ **Radishes:** Often transformed into a clever garnish, radishes are good to eat.

✔ **Salad greens (endive, escarole, lettuce, romaine, spinach):** I'm not talking anemic iceberg lettuce here, but dark, leafy greens that are full of compounds to help you resist disease.

✔ **Salsa and picante sauce:** Salsa adds pizzazz to anything!

✔ **Sauerkraut:** To retain its full flavor, sauerkraut should be served raw or barely heated through. Cooking makes kraut milder.

✔ **Snow peas:** Snow peas are excellent in salads, stir-fry, or featured on a veggie platter.

✔ **Spinach:** Tender young spinach works best in salads, either alone or mixed with other greens.

✔ **Squash, summer:** Summer squash is delicious raw or cooked.

✔ **Tomatoes, fresh:** The red color of tomatoes signals the presence of lycopene, a phytochemical that protects against cancer. Look for other tomato varieties in your market as well, including green zebra, yellow teardrop, pear, grape, and cherry. So many choices, so little time!

✔ **Tomato sauce:** Cooking doesn't destroy lycopene. It actually makes it better.

✔ **Tomato/vegetable juice:** Tomato juice, whether alone or combined with other vegetables juices, makes a great healthy drink — any time, any place.

✔ **Tomatoes, canned:** Canned tomatoes fill in nicely when fresh tomatoes are out of season.

✔ **Turnips:** Peel turnips before cooking; the peel gives a bitter flavor to the vegetable.

✔ **Water chestnuts:** Combine the crunchy, crisp vegetable with other veggies.

✔ **Watercress:** Watercress adds a distinctive flavor to salads, sandwiches, soups, and vegetables. Never overcook it — it becomes stringy when overcooked.

✔ **Zucchini:** Zucchini is a versatile green squash — cooked or raw.

Strictly speaking, a tomato is a fruit, not a vegetable. But for the purposes of this book, I'm just going to keep it in the vegetable category, where everyone expects it.

To increase your vegetable intake, try these suggestions:

✔ Pile lettuce, sprouts, and tomatoes on your sandwich.

✔ Enjoy soup or salad with a variety of vegetables.

✔ Pack zucchini slices, baby carrots, or celery sticks in your lunch.

✔ Chop raw veggies and add them to your green salad.

✔ Steam your own mixed veggie combinations with a variety of seasonings.

✔ Sauté spinach in a tiny bit of olive oil with garlic for a super quick, warm salad.

Indulging in Free Proteins

Protein is an important part of a healthy diet. Its function is to build and repair body tissues. Proteins from animal sources like meat, fish, dairy, and egg products are valued because their total protein content is high. They're referred to as *complete proteins* because they contain all the essential *amino acids* (the building blocks for constructing and repairing body tissues) required from your diet. However, many animal protein sources are also associated with saturated fat. Saturated fat contributes to heart disease by raising your cholesterol level. Choose animal proteins that are low in saturated fat.

Scientific studies show that in some people replacing some of the carbohydrate in a diet with lean protein lowers triglyceride levels and raises HDL cholesterol levels. That's good, because high triglycerides and low HDL cholesterol have been identified as risk factors for heart disease. Plus, if you eat some protein instead of carbs, you feel satisfied sooner!

Meat and cheese choices

Meat and cheese contain many good nutrients, but the fat in these foods is mostly saturated fat, and you need to limit your intake of saturated fat. Meat and cheese choices should have no more than 5 grams of fat per ounce. In the following sections, the number listed in brackets after each food is the number of grams of fat per ounce. To reduce saturated fat even further, choose the foods with 3 grams of fat per ounce, such as beef sirloin, or 0 to 1 gram of fat per ounce, such as chicken.

Beef

Lean beef is an excellent protein choice. You can eat it several times per week. Choose USDA Choice or Select grades of lean meat. Avoid heavily marbled (high-fat) meats because they're high in saturated fat.

- ✔ Corned beef [5 grams of fat per ounce]
- ✔ Flank steak [3]
- ✔ Ground beef, lean [3]
- ✔ Ground beef, regular [5]
- ✔ Prime rib [5]
- ✔ Roast (rib, chuck, rump) [3]
- ✔ Round [3]
- ✔ Short ribs [5]
- ✔ Sirloin [3]
- ✔ Steak (T-bone, porterhouse) [3]
- ✔ Tenderloin [3]

Lamb

A favorite meat around the world, the leanest cuts of lamb are leg, arm, shank, and loin.

- ✔ Chop [3 grams of fat per ounce]
- ✔ Leg [3]
- ✔ Roast [5]

Pork

Pork is a lot leaner these days and you can include it in a healthy diet. Prepackaged hams usually have only a fraction of the fat of a whole ham.

- ✔ Boston butt [5 grams of fat per ounce]
- ✔ Canadian bacon [3]
- ✔ Center loin chop [3]
- ✔ Cutlet, unbreaded [3]
- ✔ Ham (fresh, canned, cured) [3]
- ✔ Tenderloin [3]

Poultry

Lower in saturated fat than many cuts of red meat, poultry is popular and easy to prepare. Much of the fat in poultry is in the skin, so you need to remove it or buy skinless, boneless chicken or turkey. You can cook poultry with skin on and remove it before eating.

- ✔ Chicken, dark meat [3 grams of fat per ounce]
- ✔ Chicken, white meat [0–1]
- ✔ Cornish hen [0–1]
- ✔ Duck, domestic [3]
- ✔ Goose, domestic [3]
- ✔ Pheasant (no skin) [0–1]
- ✔ Turkey, dark meat [3]
- ✔ Turkey, white meat [0–1]

Veal

Veal is a favorite meat in Italy. All cuts of veal are lean; it's what we tend to do to them — breading, like Veal Parmigiana, thick butter sauces, like Veal Picatta, and so on — that make veal not so healthy.

- ✔ Chop, trimmed of visible fat [3 grams of fat per ounce]
- ✔ Cutlet (unbreaded) [3]
- ✔ Roast [3]

Cholesterol in foods is not the same as cholesterol in your blood. High levels of blood cholesterol can lead to heart disease. The saturated fat in your diet leads to high blood cholesterol more than the cholesterol in foods does.

Eggs

Previously, three eggs a week was the maximum allotted amount because egg yolks were believed to contain as much as 274 mg of cholesterol, practically filling up the daily allotment of 300 mg in one gulp. Today, an egg is known to have around 214 to 220 mg of cholesterol, allowing room in the diet for one egg a day — provided egg-lovers can keep their remaining cholesterol intake below the 300-mg-per-day benchmark.

When eating eggs, keep the rest of your diet low in saturated fat. Eggs have 5 grams of fat per ounce.

If this still seems like too much cholesterol for your diet, you may want to check out some new cholesterol-friendly egg-based products like Eggland's Best and Egg Beaters. Eggland's Best are eggs from hens that are deliberately fed a diet that lowers the eggs' cholesterol significantly, to around 180 mg per egg. Egg Beaters are made primarily from seasoned egg whites (no yolks), making them a handy choice.

The cholesterol is all in the yolk; there is none in the white. If you have the time (and don't want to spend the extra cash for the premade products), you can make your own cholesterol-free egg products. Use two egg whites and 1 teaspoon oil in place of a whole egg in a recipe. If you're making an omelet or frittata, you can probably get away without using the extra oil.

Cheese

Cheese is a nutritious food, but not a low-fat one. Most supermarkets carry reduced-fat cheeses. Try combining cheese with fresh fruit for a healthy snack or dessert.

- Cheddar, reduced-fat [5 grams of fat per ounce]
- Colby, reduced-fat [5]
- Cottage cheese, low-fat [0–1]
- Cottage cheese, regular [3]
- Feta [5]

✔ Mozzarella [5]

✔ Parmesan [3]

✔ Ricotta [5]

Note: Regular cheddar and Colby cheese have 10 grams of fat per ounce! Make sure to choose the reduced-fat variety.

Seafood

Seafood is a terrific source of protein, low in calories and low in fat. Whether you choose fish or shellfish, you're bound to get a dose of concentrated protein, all wrapped up in a light and delicate package.

 If you're not familiar with including fish in your diet, start with canned tuna and salmon. Then try broiled orange roughy, flounder, tilapia, or grilled salmon. Start ordering grilled, broiled, or baked fish and seafood in restaurants to become familiar with non-fried choices.

 Current guidelines from the American Heart Association recommend two seafood-based meals a week for all Americans. Fish is a heart-healthy food because it is high in omega-3 fatty acids.

 Omega-3 fatty acids are good fats that make your blood less likely to form clots that can cause a heart attack. Experts recommend that healthy people eat omega-3 fatty acids from fish and plant sources to protect their hearts. The fatty acids also protect against irregular heartbeat that causes sudden cardiac death. Check out Chapter 5 for more about omega-3s and other fatty acids.

Healthy adults should eat two servings a week of fish such as mackerel, lake trout, herring, sardines, albacore tuna, and salmon.

Fish

Fresh fish contains less saturated fat than red meat. Try to eat fish two to three times a week. Most markets have significantly expanded their seafood offerings. Check with your local fishmonger for his recommendations.

- Catfish [3 grams of fat per ounce]
- Cod, fresh or frozen [0–1]
- Flounder [0–1]
- Grouper[0–1]
- Haddock [0–1]
- Halibut [0–1]
- Herring, uncreamed or smoked [3]
- Mahimahi [0–1]
- Orange roughy [0–1]
- Salmon, fresh or canned [3]
- Sardines, canned [3]
- Scrod [0–1]
- Snapper [0–1]
- Sole [0–1]
- Swordfish [3]
- Trout [0–1]
- Tuna, albacore [0–1]
- Tuna, canned in oil [3]
- Tuna, canned in water [0–1]

Shellfish and mollusks

Most shellfish, if not fried, are very low in fat. Shrimp is higher in cholesterol than most other seafood but low in fat.

- Clams [0–1 grams of fat per ounce]
- Crab [0–1]
- Crawfish [0–1]
- Lobster [0–1]
- Mussels [0–1]
- Oysters, raw [0–1]
- Scallops [0–1]
- Shrimp [0–1]

Making Meals from Whole-Food Choices

Let Green Light foods be the focus of your meals. Each meal should have a lean meat, fish, or poultry, at least one serving of the free veggies, and at least one serving of the free fruits. *Remember:* You aren't held to a specific amount.

Use snacks for appetite control. I like to call this preventive eating. In other words, you eat in order not to eat. Strategically plan snacks in your day. Raw fruits and veggies make great snacks and satisfy your appetite on their own. However, I've found that the protein foods taste better with a fruit or veggie partner. Here are some examples:

- ✔ String cheese and seedless grapes
- ✔ Chicken salad with light mayonnaise and Granny Smith apples
- ✔ Lettuce-wrapped Chihuahua cheese and salsa
- ✔ Boiled shrimp and zingy tomato cocktail sauce
- ✔ Prosciutto and melon

Sounds really simple, huh? To get you started, use these easy recipes as examples of ways to incorporate the Green Light foods listed in this chapter into a varied, delicious diet. Did I mention these are free foods? That means you can eat them any time you feel like it!

Letting Green-Light Foods Satisfy Your Appetite

The trick to eating well is knowing when you've had enough but not too much. You probably recognize that stuffed feeling, and you certainly know when you're still hungry. You also know that both of these states are uncomfortable.

To get a better sense of when you've had enough to eat, but not too much, follow these suggestions:

✔ **Slow it down.** Your stomach needs 15 minutes to tell your brain that you're full. Eat slowly and let your brain catch up!

✔ **Forget counting calories.** Focus on feeling satisfied with proper foods instead of targeting a specific calorie value. If you don't feel full, eat more fruits, non-starchy vegetables, or lean protein foods rather than sweets and junk foods.

✔ **Prepare yourself mentally for making changes in your diet, then set a start date.**

✔ **Eat regular meals — three meals, three to four hours apart, with three food groups at each meal.**

✔ **Plan snacks of Green Light foods.**

✔ **Divide your plate into quarters and fill three quarters with Green Light foods.**

✔ **Drink six to eight 8-ounce glasses of water per day.**

✔ **Follow this plan 90 percent of the time, and treat yourself to a favorite food 10 percent of the time.**

The health benefits of eating more fruits and vegetables

You can reduce your risk of coronary heart disease, stroke, and obesity by increasing your consumption of vegetables and fruit. In addition, some scientific studies have demonstrated that greater fruit and vegetable consumption is consistent with a reduced risk of some types of cancers, including cancer of the stomach, esophagus, and lungs. The types of vegetables that most often appear to be protective against cancer are raw vegetables, followed by *allium* vegetables (onions, garlic, scallions, leeks, chives), carrots, green vegetables, *cruciferous* vegetables (broccoli, cauliflower, Brussels sprouts, cabbage), and tomatoes.

Chapter 5

Navigating Your Way through Carbs, Proteins, and Fats

● ●

In This Chapter

▶ Understanding refined carbohydrate foods

▶ Choosing the healthiest starchy carbohydrate foods

▶ Knowing what you stand to gain from dairy foods

▶ Recognizing the importance of calcium in your diet

▶ Knowing the importance of fat in the diet

▶ Understanding the different kinds of fat

▶ Choosing the best food sources of fat

▶ Knowing how much fat to eat

● ●

*P*oor misunderstood carbohydrate. First it was good, and then it was bad. I don't blame you if you're frustrated and confused when it comes to carbs.

Of all the many functions of carbohydrate foods, in this chapter I want you to keep one main function in mind: Carbohydrate is fuel. You've probably heard carbs described as a quick-energy food. A lot of people think what that means is, "If I eat carbs, I'll feel more energetic." For most people, that's not exactly true. Marathon runners often eat a lot of pasta before a big race because they need a quick energy source to fuel their muscles for their long run ahead. But, if you're going to sit or stand on the sidelines to cheer them on, you don't need a lot of pasta. And if you aren't going to burn the fuel, then you'll store the fuel. And guess how that fuel is stored? You got it — as the dreaded body fat.

I also fill you in on the importance of dairy foods in your diet, focusing in particular on the benefits of calcium (and the risks you face if you aren't getting enough of it).

Plus, guess what? Fats are back, and some of them are even good for you — so good for you, in fact, that you should eat *more* of them. So, I tell you about two different (but very much related) concepts: fat, the nutrient, that functions in your body, and dietary fat that you eat, which may help or hurt your body. I show you how fats that naturally occur in some foods are actually very healthy for you *and* your heart. I introduce you to fats that are absolutely delicious and fun to eat — they not only satisfy your appetite, but also improve your health.

Yellow Light: Putting Starchy Carbs on Cruise Control

In the Whole Foods Eating Plan, certain fruits and vegetables are classified as Green Light, meaning "Go, go, go, and eat all you want." These foods are listed in detail in Chapter 4. There *are* carbohydrates in these foods, but they're not counted in the Whole Foods Eating Plan, because the carbs are usually low on the glycemic load index and are very healthy for you. Carbohydrate that comes from starchy food sources is called Yellow Light, meaning "Exercise caution." Be careful not to eat too much of these foods, because you can only have five choices a day. Occasionally, you can substitute a refined or sweet carb for one or two of your starchy carbs.

Controlling your intake of the starchy carbs outlined in this section is a key component of the Whole Foods Eating Plan. This is the feature of the plan that allows for weight loss and lowers your triglycerides, blood sugar, and blood pressure if they're elevated. You may have five carbohydrate choices per day. A carbohydrate choice is a serving that supplies 15 grams of total carbohydrate — for example, 3 cups of low-fat microwave popcorn or ½ cup of beans. Try to choose the healthiest foods in this category (for example, whole-grain breads and cereals or dried beans and peas).

Because you live in the real world and not just in the pages of this book, the plan is designed to also let you have an occasional sweet treat or snack food. Don't fall into the trap of saying, "I won't eat any of the Yellow Light foods. I can just eat the Green Light foods." Doing so puts you at risk of insufficient carbohydrate for your needs. Plus, you'll be eliminating some very important healthy foods from your diet.

Always eat at least three servings of carbs, but no more than five servings from this group per day. Check out the next section for information on how much constitutes a serving.

Controlling Portion Sizes

The key to enjoying carbohydrates while maintaining a low-carb lifestyle is portion control. The Yellow Light foods are not free foods like the delicious cornucopia detailed in Chapter 4. They're categorized as Yellow Light because you need to exercise caution and keep them under control. Exceeding the serving size of a lot of the foods in this category is easy to do.

 ✔ **Breads:** Bread is an important part of any healthy diet, even a low-carb one. Over the years, many people have increased their intake of bread because it's low in fat, despite being fairly high in carbs. But the important thing to consider when choosing bread is the type of grain used to make it. Refined-grain breads, like everyday white bread, are soft, smooth-textured, and very tasty. However, refining the grain eliminates a lot of nutrients and increases the glycemic load of the bread, meaning your body converts these carbs to glucose very quickly; thus, you aren't satisfied for long and get hungrier quicker. Whole-grain breads are more nutritious and lower on the glycemic index chart; they affect your blood sugar more slowly and leave you feeling full longer.

Quinoa: The super "grain"

Quinoa (KEEN-wah) isn't exactly a grain, but this wonder food cooks like a grain, tastes like a grain, quacks like a grain. . . . You get the picture. Quinoa is actually a seed that is packed full of protein (including the all-important amino acid, lysine), calcium, and B-complex vitamins, including folic acid.

Quinoa is a wonder food with at least as complete a protein as whole milk, and about as many carbs. Relatively new to North America, quinoa sustained the South American Incas, dating back at least 5,000 years. The seed itself closely resembles millet and comes in a variety of colors, ranging from red, orange, and yellow to white and black.

Before arriving at your grocery-store shelves, the seeds are processed to remove their bitter saponin coating. Unlike traditional refining, this process does not diminish the nutritional value of the quinoa; it simply makes it palatable.

You can find quinoa in most health-food stores and many larger grocery stores.

Choose whole-grain rolls, muffins, and bread products to stay fuller longer. For more on glycemic index and glycemic load, see Chapter 2. For more information on the benefits of whole grains and fiber in your diet, take a look at "Choosing the Best, Leaving the Rest," later in this chapter.

The more refined a grain is, the fewer the vitamins and minerals and the higher the glycemic load. When you eat these refined foods, they quickly turn to blood sugar. Choose whole, intact grain foods, such as wheat, rye, and barley. They're a major source of cereal fiber and contain numerous phytochemicals that can lower your risk of heart disease, diabetes, and cancer. Eat a minimum of three servings per day.

✔ **Cereals, grains, and pasta:** The principle of whole grains applies here. Choose whole-grain cereals with no added sugar and whole-wheat pasta. Each serving of these foods equals approximately 15 grams of total carbohydrate (or one serving).

To bump up your intake of whole-grain foods, look for one of the following ingredients *first* on the food label's ingredient list:

- Brown rice
- Oatmeal
- Whole oats
- Bulgur
- Popcorn
- Whole rye
- Cracked wheat
- Whole barley
- Whole wheat
- Graham flour
- Whole cornmeal

Try some of these whole-grain foods:

- Whole-wheat bread
- Whole-grain ready-to-eat cereal
- Low-fat whole-wheat crackers
- Oatmeal
- Corn tortillas
- Whole-wheat pasta
- Whole barley in soup
- Tabouli salad

Wheat flour, enriched flour, and degerminated corn meal are not whole grains. Most basic all-purpose or white flour comes from wheat; it's just refined and less healthy. And just because the bread is brown does not mean it's whole-grain. Some food manufacturers just add color to white bread to make it look like whole wheat.

✔ **Vegetables and fruit:** Starchy vegetables are delicious and you're not alone if you love them. The white Russet potato, a big crowd-pleaser, is particularly high in glycemic load. Enjoy these vegetables, but watch the portion size and count them appropriately as part of your five carbohydrate choices.

Food	Amount to Equal One Serving
Baked beans	⅓ cup
Banana	1 small (6 inches long)
Corn	½ cup
Corn on the cob, medium	1 ear
Mixed vegetables with corn, peas, or pasta	1 cup
Peas, green (English peas)	½ cup
Plantain	½ cup
Potato, baked or boiled	1 small
Potato, mashed	½ cup
Squash, winter (acorn, butternut)	1 cup
Yam or sweet potato, plain	½ cup

The banana is one fruit I put on the starch list, because it has a higher starch content than other fruits. Bananas are the number-one fruit sold in the United States, and many people who eat bananas tend to eat a lot of them. So enjoy them occasionally, but be sure to think of them as a carbohydrate. If you have been told by your doctor to eat bananas for potassium, be aware that you can get just as much potassium from your Green Light fruits and vegetables, such as cantaloupe, orange or grapefruit juice, honeydew, watermelon, raisins, broccoli, spinach, summer squash, and tomatoes.

✔ **Dried beans, peas, and lentils:** Dried beans and peas contain a fair amount of protein and are often counted as a meat substitute. They're low in glycemic load and can contain as many as 8 grams of dietary fiber per serving.

If you don't eat animal products, but you want to follow a low-carb diet, use this group of Yellow Light foods as your Green Light proteins. If you have no meat, fish, or poultry at a meal, the legumes and soy products count as protein, not starch. However, if animal meat is included, you have to count these products as starch.

Oh, soy good!

You've probably heard a little something about soy. Whether it's soy supplements for menopausal and premenopausal women, or good press about the Asian diet, soy is making more news than ever these days.

Soy foods are packed full of great things including protein, carbs, calcium, vitamins, omega-3 fatty acids, and fiber. You name it, it's probably in there. The protein in soy is complete, meaning it has all eight essential amino acids.

Soy is packed full of antioxidants and isoflavones, which are powerful health-promoting compounds. Soy is believed to help reduce the risk of cardiovascular disease, by helping to lower LDL ("bad") cholesterol, and some kinds of cancer, including breast, prostate, and uterine cancer.

Soy estrogens are helping to alleviate menopausal symptoms for many women. Preliminary research indicates that soy foods are particularly good for diabetics at risk or experiencing symptoms of kidney disease.

If you haven't taken the plunge, try fitting soy products into your diet. Tofu may not sound appealing to you, but the best thing about it (besides the obvious nutrition) is that it takes on the flavor of whatever your cook it in or with. It's great in soups and sauce. Crumble a little in spaghetti sauce or chili.

Or you may prefer to try a type of soy that's completely different like edamame, miso, soy nuts, or soy milk. So rather than replace meat with tofu, just add soy products to your diet.

Currently, there is no official Recommended Daily Allowance (RDA) for soy protein, but many food producers are calling out soy protein grams separately on their food labels.

✔ **Crackers and snacks:** This is a category of food that has gotten completely out of hand in the American diet. Most of these foods are made from refined flour and are low in vitamins and minerals. Think about how frequently you choose these foods and try to substitute fresh fruit and veggies for your snack. When you do choose these foods, keep in mind that one serving equals approximately 15 grams of total carbohydrate.

To keep from overeating snack foods, take out the portion you need and then put the bag or box away. That way, you won't reach into a large bag of snacks and continue eating until the bag is empty. Try to include raw fruit, veggies, or low-fat cheese with your snack.

Check out soy nuts if you haven't tried them. You get one and a half to two times the quantity compared to other snacks, plus you add calcium, protein, soy, and dietary fiber wrapped up in a snack-food package. Look for these in the snack-food aisle in many flavors — chile-lime, salt, teriyaki, and even barbecue.

Choosing the Best, Leaving the Rest

A good rule for making your carbohydrate selection each day is to stick to low-glycemic-load foods as often as possible. Choose whole grains for at least three of your carb choices and legumes for the other two for the healthiest diet.

✓ **Low-glycemic-load carbs:** Foods with a low glycemic load affect your blood sugar slowly. Here are some examples of low-glycemic-load carbs and their serving sizes:

- ½ cup of beans or peas (garbanzo, pinto, kidney, white, split, black-eyed)

- ⅔ cup of lima beans

- 1 slice of high-fiber bread (rye, whole-wheat, multigrain)

- ¾ ounce (2 to 5) whole-wheat crackers

- 3 cups of low-fat microwave popcorn

Whole-grain foods fall into the lower-glycemic-load category because they slow the digestion of starches into the bloodstream. These foods also have many other nutritional benefits, including the following:

- They improve the health of the gastrointestinal tract by improving regularity.

- They lower the risk of mouth, stomach, colon, gallbladder, and ovarian cancer.

- They reduce LDL ("bad") cholesterol, while maintaining HDL ("good") cholesterol.

- They may reduce some kinds of heart disease.

- They contain valuable *phytochemicals* (naturally occurring plant-based chemicals that help fight disease).

- They contain essential vitamins and minerals.

✔ **High-glycemic-load carbs:** High-glycemic-load carbs quickly affect your blood sugar and may leave you hungrier more quickly than their low-glycemic-load counterparts. Starchy veggies with a high glycemic load like potatoes can be part of your plan and add to your daily fiber intake as long as you eat them in moderation.

Whenever possible, eat your starchy vegetables, like potatoes, with the skin in tact. You're sure to get the most nutrients and an extra dose of dietary fiber. Don't go crazy and start eating banana peels and spaghetti squash hulls, because that's just, well, silly — but eating a russet potato skin now and then won't hurt you.

Here are some examples of carbohydrate choices with a higher glycemic load:

- 1 slice white bread

- ½ cup of macaroni, spaghetti, or rice

- ½ cup of potatoes

- ¾ cup of unsweetened, ready-to-eat cereal

- 6 saltine crackers

- 5 vanilla wafers

Putting the Brakes on Refined Carbs

Refined carbs are foods that are highly processed and pre-packaged, like chips, cookies, cakes, candy, crackers, and bread. They may even have enticing packaging, claiming to be fat-free or cholesterol-free. But be very discriminating and read your nutrition labels so you know exactly what you're eating. (See Chapter 7 for more information on reading food labels the low-carb way.)

Refined carbohydrates have a low nutrient density, meaning their nutrient value is low compared to the number of calories they pack. Many of these foods have become popular because they're low in fat. People see them as free foods because of their low fat grams, a big mistake.

Trading off your carb choices for an occasional treat

Say that you're at a coworker's birthday party. You're handed a piece of birthday cake and you want to eat it. If it's a normal size serving of birthday cake, just count it as two carb choices and go on about your day. *Remember:* On the Whole Foods Eating Plan, you can still eat your Green Light fruits, veggies, and lean proteins after you've had your five carbs choices for the day. See Chapter 4 for more info on the Whole Foods Eating Plan.

Paying attention to sugar

You can eat sweets and sugar, if you count the carbohydrate they contain. The problem is that sugars and sweets don't have vitamins or minerals, and they do have a lot of calories, even in small servings. My best recommendation is to avoid hidden sugars in food, especially refined, pre-packaged, and processed foods. Make the sugar you eat count. Did you really enjoy that fat-free cookie? Probably not, but it likely contained 12 grams of carbs, which is equivalent to eating an entire *tablespoon* of sugar. You'd probably be more satisfied with ¾ cup of fresh strawberries, which contain the same number of carbs, have way more fiber and nutrients, and are pretty darn filling. And don't forget, strawberries are free to you — whereas the fat-free cookie will cost you one carb choice for the day.

Avoiding the urge to exceed your daily allowance

The best way to avoid exceeding the carb allowance is to build your meals around the Green Light foods. Always think of those free fruits and veggies first because the amounts are unlimited. Also track your portion sizes of carb choice foods.

Overeating of a particular food is often a habit. It's surprising
how satisfying a smaller portion can be, especially if you eat
it with a variety of unlimited foods. If nothing seems to abate
that sweet craving, then indulge it with a controlled amount.
Eat it slowly, savor it, and then get back on track.

Fitting in Your Daily Dietary Fiber

Fiber is an important contribution from many of the foods
in this group. Soluble fiber is helpful in lowering your cholesterol and comes from whole grains like oats, barley, and rye
and also from dried beans and peas. Insoluble fiber is helpful
in lowering your risk of colon cancer and other cancers of the
gastrointestinal tract. Whole grains on the average provide
3 grams of dietary fiber per serving. Specialty cereals designed
to provide more fiber (for example, Bran Flakes, All Bran, Fiber
One) can provide 8 to 13 grams of dietary fiber per serving.
Dried beans and peas can provide up to 8 grams of dietary
fiber per serving. If you carefully select foods from this group,
you can get the dietary fiber per day that your body needs.

If you can't get excited about ½ cup of All-Bran or Fiber One,
mix them with ½ to ¾ cup Cheerios or Wheaties for two carb
servings and 15 grams of fiber. Add 1 cup fresh strawberries
and 1 cup skim milk. You still have only used 2 carb choices
and your fiber intake is 19 grams for one meal.

Putting It on the Menu: The Daily Plan

As a rule, the best way to spend your five carb choices is to
pick three of them from the whole-grains family (like whole-
wheat crackers or whole-grain bread) and two of them from
the legume group (like black beans or lentils) for the fiber. On
occasion, you can definitely work in potatoes and bananas
and so on. But really work on improving your intake of whole
grains and legumes. You'll see results in both weight loss and
general good health.

Understanding the Benefits of Dairy Foods

Dairy foods such as milk, yogurt, cheese, and ice cream contain carbohydrate in the form of a milk sugar called *lactose*. Lactose is the principal carbohydrate of milk, making up about 5 percent of its weight. Lactose contributes 30 to 50 percent of milk's energy, depending on the milk's fat content. However, milk, yogurt, and other dairy products are low in glycemic load, so you can include them in your lower-carbohydrate meal plan. You should eat two to three servings per day and you do not count them as a carbohydrate choice on the Whole Foods Eating Plan. Check out Chapter 4 for an overview of the eating plan.

The fact that dairy products are low in glycemic load is a good thing, because eating dairy foods has been demonstrated to reduce *hypertension* (high blood pressure), and the risk of osteoporosis, kidney stones, and colon cancer. The fat in dairy products is mostly saturated fat, which can increase the risk of heart disease, but very-low-fat dairy foods and nonfat dairy foods allow you to have all the benefits without the fat. These dairy foods are also rich sources of vital nutrients that can prevent disease.

Got milk? Got nutrients

Dairy foods are excellent sources of calcium, phosphorous, riboflavin, protein, magnesium, vitamin A, vitamin B_6, and vitamin B_{12}. If fortified (and most milk *is* fortified), milk provides appreciable amounts of vitamin D as well.

So what does this mean for your body? Take a look at just some of the benefits you stand to gain from the nutrients found in dairy products:

- **Phosphorus:** This is an important mineral in bones and teeth and a part of every cell in the body.

- **Riboflavin:** This vitamin supports normal vision and healthy skin. It's important to the production of energy in your body.

Lactose intolerance

Lactose intolerance occurs when the body doesn't make enough of an enzyme called *lactase*. Lactase breaks down lactose (milk sugar) found in dairy foods. When people don't have enough lactase, they may have a problem digesting dairy products. Soon after eating or drinking dairy products, they may experience gas, bloating, stomach cramps, and/or diarrhea. If you're lactose intolerant, you can control the symptoms through simple changes in your diet.

If you avoid dairy products, you may not be getting enough calcium and vitamin D. Both are necessary for healthy bones and the prevention of osteoporosis, a disease that weakens bones and causes them to break easily. To make sure you're getting enough calcium, try these tips:

✔ **Don't give up on dairy entirely.** People who have trouble digesting lactose can often tolerate milk with meals. Start with small ½-cup servings and gradually increase the size of servings. Always drink milk with food; dairy products may be better digested if eaten with other foods, so eat dairy foods with a meal. Try eating smaller quantities of dairy more often; you may be able to

tolerate small amounts of dairy better than a large amount all at once. Eat cheese, which is lower in lactose; aged hard cheeses like Colby, cheddar, Swiss, and parmesan have less lactose than softer cheeses. (Try low-fat versions of these cheeses.) Try yogurt and milk with active cultures, which produce lactase and are often easier to tolerate.

✔ **Look for lactose-free or lactose-reduced dairy foods in your supermarket.**

✔ **Try adding lactase to your food.** Lactase comes in a liquid form, chewable tablets, and capsules. You can buy lactase at your pharmacy without a prescription.

✔ **Eat soy products, which are great sources of calcium.** Try calcium-fortified soy milk, tofu, soy yogurt, and soy nuts.

✔ **Eat lots of dark green leafy vegetables like broccoli, collard greens, kale, turnip greens, mustard greens, and bok choy, all of which are a good source of calcium.**

✔ **Try calcium-fortified juices and calcium-fortified cereals.**

✔ **Protein:** This nutrient builds and repairs body tissues.

✔ **Magnesium:** This mineral is important in building healthy bones and teeth. It's also important in muscle contractions and nerve impulses.

✓ **Vitamin A:** This is an important vitamin in maintaining healthy eyes and skin. It is also important in bone and tooth growth.

✓ **Vitamin B$_6$:** This vitamin helps make red blood cells and helps build proteins in your body.

✓ **Vitamin B$_{12}$:** This vitamin prevents anemia and helps maintain healthy nerve cells.

✓ **Vitamin D:** This vitamin helps maintain calcium and phosphorus for healthy bones.

If you were paying attention, you may have noticed calcium missing from that list. That's because the following section is devoted to the benefits of calcium (and what happens to your body if you don't get enough of it).

Calcium: It's everywhere!

Calcium is found in great abundance in the human body, and 99 percent of it is found in the bones and teeth. (That's why, when kids are growing, they need calcium to build strong bones and teeth.) But where is that remaining 1 percent of calcium found? In the blood. Calcium plays important roles in nerve conduction, muscle contraction, and blood clotting.

Knowing how much calcium you need

If calcium levels in the blood drop below normal, your body will pull calcium from your bones and put it into the blood in order to maintain the blood calcium levels it needs. If your blood borrows too much calcium from your bones, you're at risk for lots of conditions related to calcium deficiency, including osteoporosis. Consuming enough calcium throughout your lifetime, whether you're a man or a woman, is important in order to maintain adequate blood and bone calcium levels.

The National Institute of Health Consensus Conference and the National Osteoporosis Foundation recommend a higher calcium intake of 1,500 mg per day for postmenopausal women not taking estrogen and men and women 65 years or older. Talk to your doctor or registered dietitian about the amount of calcium that's right for you.

Vitamin D and calcium: Their critical connection

Most foods that are fortified with calcium are also fortified with vitamin D. Vitamin D is a critical piece in the calcium-absorption puzzle. It enables your body to use the calcium you're taking in. Additionally, vitamin D helps your body reabsorb calcium in the kidneys rather than allow it to be removed from the body with waste. Vitamin D also helps your body maintain a proper balance of calcium and phosphorous in the bloodstream.

Current guidelines indicate that most people need between 200 and 600 IU (international units) of Vitamin D daily, depending on their age. Vitamin D supplements are usually not necessary because vitamin D is available from fortified milk and foods such as fish and egg yolks.

Vitamin D is also known as "the sunshine vitamin." You only need 15 minutes of sunlight exposure without sunscreen each day to maintain an adequate vitamin D level. The amount of skin exposed to the sun should be the equivalent of your face and arms. Sunscreens with an *SPF* (skin protection factor) of 8 or higher will block vitamin D absorption. Persons living in climates with year round cloudiness blocking the sun's rays will have less vitamin D absorption.

Vitamin D has been shown to produce adverse side effects such as *calcification* (hardening) of soft tissues (blood vessels, heart, lungs, kidneys, tissues around joints) at above 50 mcg or 2,000 IU a day.

Although calcium offers many benefits, the old adage "If some is good, more is better" most definitely does not apply. If you take more than 2,500 mg of calcium per day, you may experience adverse side effects. High calcium intakes can lead to constipation and an increased chance of developing calcium kidney stones; it may also inhibit your absorption of iron and zinc, both of which are vital nutrients your body needs. Calcium supplements are better absorbed in divided doses. So, don't take 1200 mg all at one time. Divide it into 600 mg in the morning and 600 mg at night.

If you're a nursing mother whose doctor or lactation consultant has recommended that you cut back on your intake of dairy products because they're upsetting your baby's stomach, make sure you still get at least your minimum calcium requirement from non-dairy sources and supplements. Sufficient calcium in your diet is essential in order to provide proper nutrition for you and your baby.

Recognizing what can happen if you don't get enough calcium

Everybody needs calcium, but as you age you need even more because your body naturally loses calcium *and* has a much tougher time absorbing it. Talk about a double whammy! Although dairy foods are a rich source of calcium, you can also get calcium from oranges, broccoli, dried beans, soy, spinach, and canned salmon with bones.

Calcium can play a major role in disease prevention. Three good reasons to count on calcium are the prevention of osteoporosis, high blood pressure, and colon cancer.

- ✔ **Osteoporosis:** *Osteoporosis* means "porous bone." It's a disease characterized by a decrease in bone mineral density and bone calcium content and leads to an increased risk of fractures. One out of two women and one out of eight men will develop osteoporosis. A diet high in calcium can help slow bone loss. Preserving bone mass helps reduce your risk of developing this bone-thinning and debilitating disease.

- ✔ **High blood pressure:** As many as 50 million Americans have high blood pressure (also referred to as *hypertension*). High blood pressure increases your risk of heart disease, stroke, and kidney disease. Calcium, potassium, and magnesium are three nutrients shown to reduce blood pressure. Potassium and magnesium help calcium lower blood pressure. Dairy foods contain ample amounts of all three of these nutrients. Getting all these nutrients in your diet can reduce your systolic blood pressure (the top number in a blood pressure measurement) by 8 to 14 points. Adding exercise will reduce it 4 to 9 points more.

- ✔ **Colon cancer:** Colon cancer is the third leading cause of cancer deaths in the United States. A recent study showed that people who consume at least a moderate amount of calcium in their diet (700 to 800 mg per day) significantly reduced their risk of colon cancer by 40 to 50 percent. Boosting your calcium intake, along with consuming a high-fiber diet, may help reduce your risk.

Getting enough calcium

The fat in dairy foods contains a high ratio of saturated fat, and high saturated fat intake has consistently been linked to high cholesterol levels and heart disease. Reducing your saturated fat intake as much as possible is a good idea.

Opt for low-fat or fat-free milk, yogurt, and cheese whenever possible. They contain fewer calories and little to no saturated fat but all the vitamins and minerals that the higher-fat versions contain.

Children under 2 years of age need quite a bit of fat in their diet for adequate brain and nerve development, so they should drink whole milk instead of the low-fat or fat-free versions.

Two to three servings per day of fat-free or low-fat dairy foods are allowed on the Whole Foods Eating Plan. However, based on new evidence and a person's individual risk for osteoporosis, three to four servings may be more appropriate for some people. A serving is 1 cup of skim milk, 1 to 1½ ounces of cheese, or 6 to 8 ounces of yogurt.

Recognizing How Fat Helps Your Body

Fat has negative connotations for many people, but in the body, fat is an essential nutrient. In fact, fat, in moderate amounts, is *necessary* for your health. In this section, I show you how fat helps your body.

> ✓ **Regulating body processes:** All humans need fat in order to maintain healthy skin and regulate cholesterol metabolism. Fat is also necessary for the formation of hormone-like substances called *prostaglandins,* which regulate many body processes such as your body's inflammation response to injury and infection as well as blood vessel contractions and nerve impulses. The fat-soluble vitamins A, D, E, and K, stored in your body fat, play many specific roles in the growth and maintenance of your body.

✔ **Providing energy:** Fat is a concentrated source of energy for the body by providing 9 calories per gram (compared with 4 calories per gram from either carbohydrates or protein). Fat is an important calorie source especially for infants and young children; 50 percent of the calories in human breast milk come from fat. Some storage of energy in your body in the form of fat is essential to your health.

✔ **Storing it up:** The body uses whatever fat it needs for energy, and the rest is stored in various fatty tissues. Some fat is found in blood plasma and other body cells, but the largest amount is stored in the body's fat cells. These fat deposits not only act as storage for energy, but also are important in insulating the body and supporting and cushioning organs.

Understanding the Different Kinds of Fat

Many people assume that dietary fat is directly connected with body fat and heart disease, but that isn't exactly true. Some studies show that women who eat the least amount of fat are the most overweight. As far as heart disease, some fats actually *protect* the heart, while others can certainly be harmful. So, just as not all carbohydrates are created equal, not all fats are created equal. Knowing the differences between the various kinds of fat and identifying where they're found in the foods you eat is key.

The fat in food is often referred to as saturated, monounsaturated, and polyunsaturated, but no dietary fat is 100 percent of any of those categories. Dietary fat is classified by the fatty acid that is present in the greatest quantity. For example, olive oil contains 13 percent saturated fat, 72 percent monounsaturated fat, and 8 percent polyunsaturated fat. Because it contains more monounsaturated fat than anything else, it is classified as a monounsaturated fat.

HDL is "good" cholesterol. It helps keep the arteries clear by picking up fatty fragments and taking them back to the liver where they are degraded. LDL is "bad" cholesterol. This type of cholesterol sticks to your arteries and forms plaque; the result can be reduced blood flow or the formation of a clot that totally blocks blood flow in an artery.

Saturated fats

Saturated fatty acids are usually solid at room temperature, and they're more stable than other types of fats — that is, they don't turn rancid as quickly. Saturated fatty acids raise blood cholesterol, especially the LDL or "bad" cholesterol. Your risk of coronary heart disease rises as your blood cholesterol level increases.

The fat in meat is considered mostly saturated. You can see the visible fat of a piece of prime rib when it's served. You've probably noticed that when the juices that cook out of a roast start to cool, part of the fat starts to solidify and rise to the top. That fat that rises to the top is saturated fat.

Trans fats are a subclass of saturated fat, but they started out as an unsaturated fat like vegetable oil. Food producers and snack makers *hydrogenated* (or added hydrogen to) the vegetable oils. Hydrogenated vegetable oils are used in all kinds of common, everyday food products, such as fast food, French fries, stick margarine, and cookies.

Limiting saturated fats in your diet basically means avoiding high-fat red meats and whole-fat dairy products. Eliminating all the saturated fat in your diet isn't necessary. Eating saturated fats in the right proportion with unsaturated fats — at least 2 to 1 (unsaturated to saturated) — is perfectly fine. What that means for you is this:

✔ Reduce the saturated fat in your diet as much as possible and always eat at least twice as much unsaturated fat as you eat saturated.

✔ Eat only lean or extra-lean red meat.

✔ Only eat skim or very-low-fat dairy products.

✔ Eat more nuts and seeds.

✔ Try to eat fish two times per week.

✔ Use olive, canola, or peanut oils.

✔ Eat more olives and avocados.

Keep in mind that at least 50 percent of the trans fats you eat are hidden in commercially baked goods (like crackers, muffins, and cookies), in other prepared foods, and in fried foods prepared in restaurants.

Monounsaturated fats

Monounsaturated oils are liquid at room temperature but start to solidify at refrigerator temperatures. This is why salad dressing containing olive oil turns cloudy when refrigerated but is clear at room temperature — olive oil is a monounsaturated fat. Likewise, the fat in natural peanut butter is mostly unsaturated. If you let a jar of natural peanut butter sit for a while, you'll notice an oily layer forms on the top. That liquid is peanut oil, which is unsaturated fat and a liquid at room temperature.

Monounsaturated fatty acids lower blood cholesterol. They lower the LDL ("bad") cholesterol, and increase the HDL ("good") cholesterol (which is a good thing). They also seem to lower triglycerides in some people when substituted for carbohydrate in the diet.

You can get your daily supply of monounsaturated fats from a variety of naturally occurring food sources including almonds, avocados, canola oil, cashews, olive oil, olives, peanut butter, peanut oil, peanuts, pecans, sesame seeds, and tahini paste made from sesame seeds.

Polyunsaturated fats

Polyunsaturated oils are liquid at room temperature and in the refrigerator. They easily combine with oxygen in the air to become rancid.

Polyunsaturated fatty acids help lower total blood cholesterol — by lowering the LDL ("bad") cholesterol but not the HDL ("good") cholesterol. The primary sources of polyunsaturated fat are margarine (the tub or squeeze kind, but not stick), English walnuts, corn oil, safflower oil, soybean oil, reduced-fat salad dressings, and mayonnaise.

Omega-3 fatty acids are a special class of polyunsaturated fatty acids found primarily in fish and fish oils but can also be found in flaxseed, walnuts, and soy and canola oils. Studies suggest these fatty acids may help reduce your risk of heart disease, stroke, and cancer. We know that omega-3 fatty acids lower LDL ("bad") cholesterol and triglycerides. Great sources of omega-3 fatty acids include salmon, albacore tuna, trout, herring, mackerel, flaxseeds, walnuts, canola oil, and non-hydrogenated soybean oil.

Omega-6 fatty acids are another class of polyunsaturated fatty acids. Linoleic acid comprises the majority of the polyunsaturated fat eaten in the United States and comes from a variety of commonly consumed animal and vegetable products, like corn, safflower, sunflower, and cottonseed oils.

Knowing How Much Fat Is Enough

One serving of fat contains 45 calories and 5 grams of fat. For the average healthy adult, eight fat servings per day are appropriate. And most of those servings (at least six) should be unsaturated fat. That means more avocados but less mayonnaise; more nuts and olives but fewer full-fat dairy products; more fish and poultry; and only lean red meats.

So how do you keep your fat intake on track? Try the following suggestions:

- ✔ Avoid saturated fat, which is animal fat found in red meat and full-fat dairy products, by eating lean meats, skim milk, and low-fat cheeses.

- ✔ Eat more nuts, legumes, poultry, and fish.

- ✔ Use nonstick cooking spray and liquid and spray margarine, soft tub margarines, and margarine blends with yogurt.

Including More Healthy Fat in Your Diet

Replacing fats in the diet with refined carbohydrate creates new health problems; replacing saturated fat in the diet with unsaturated fat in the diet promotes better health. With a few simple changes, you can benefit from this proven eating plan.

Is butter better than margarine?

The potential cholesterol-raising effects of trans fatty acids have raised concern about the use of margarine and whether other options, including butter, may be better choices. Some stick margarines contribute more trans fatty acids than unhydrogenated oils or other fats.

Butter is rich in both saturated fat and cholesterol. That means it can cause the arteries to be blocked. Most margarine is made from vegetable fat and provides no dietary cholesterol. The more liquid the margarine (in tub or liquid form), the less hydrogenated it is and the fewer trans fatty acids it contains.

✔ Use liquid vegetable oils in cooking and at the table. Dipping bread in olive oil flavored with black pepper and coarse sea salt is a much better health choice than slathering it with butter.

✔ Don't let fat dominate your food intake, but sneak good fats in. When making a salad, add sliced olives instead of cheddar cheese. Toss in some sliced almonds instead of bacon with your green beans. Don't increase your total fat intake, but do change the type of fat you eat.

✔ Use olive oil as a replacement for the saturated fat in your diet. Olive oil makes all food more flavorful, fresh-tasting, and delicious. It's a natural choice for good health. Olive oil contains no cholesterol, chemicals, or artificial additives. It's especially high in monounsaturated fat, which may reduce harmful LDL cholesterol and help maintain healthy HDL cholesterol levels when substituted for saturated fat.

Improving Your Ratio of Good Fats to Bad Fats

Moderate, don't eliminate your fat intake. Mix up the kinds of fat you eat. Deliberately lower your saturated fat intake, but add more unsaturated fat, especially olive oil, peanut oil, canola oil, fish, olives, avocadoes, nuts, and nut oils. Eat two fish meals each week to increase your chances of getting omega-3 fatty acids in your diet.

Try to balance your intake of omega-3 and omega-6 fatty acids. Eat more fatty fish (salmon, albacore tuna, trout, herring, and mackerel), canola oil, flaxseed, and walnuts. Eat less corn, safflower, sunflower, and cottonseed oils.

Flaxseed contains high amounts of cancer fighters, as well as omega-3 fatty acids, which may help prevent heart disease. It also supplies iron, niacin, phosphorous, and vitamin E. To release the health benefits of flaxseed, the hard outer coating must be broken down. Place flaxseed in a small nonstick skillet; cook over low heat 5 minutes or until toasted, stirring constantly. Place the flaxseed in a blender; process just until chopped. Flaxseed keeps best when stored in the refrigerator. Toast and chop right before using.

Here are some other ways to improve your ratio of good fats to bad fats:

✔ **Try a few nuts for a snack.** But remember that 1 cup of nuts is about 800 calories, so don't eat too many!

✔ **Use thin slices of avocado in place of mayonnaise.**

✔ **Always use the reduced-fat version of a high-fat food.**

✔ **Combine cheese with fruit to lower the fat percentage for the whole snack.**

✔ **Avoid trans fats whenever possible.** Watch for ingredients like partially hydrogenated fat. Choose tub over stick margarine. Avoid shortening, commercially prepared breads, pastries, cookies, and French fries.

Chapter 6

Yes, You Can: Setting Yourself Up to Succeed

*I*s your home your own worst enemy? Chances are, some of your greatest temptations are right in your own kitchen. The typical kitchen tends to have too many high-calorie, high-carbohydrate, and high-fat foods and too few fruits and vegetables, whole grains, lean meats, and low-fat dairy products.

You need to build an environment that supports your new healthy lifestyle. You may be tempted to give the whole place an overhaul. But your spouse and kids or other housemates may be saying, "We aren't changing the way we eat. Don't get rid of *our* food." You don't have to toss out everyone's favorite food. Think about giving your kitchen a makeover rather than an overhaul. Tolerate some high-calorie foods in the house, but focus on eating healthier snacks. Make those healthy choices available to everyone. You may be surprised at how often other family members choose a healthy food when they have a choice.

Identifying Your Trigger Foods

Each of us has our own high-calorie foods that we just can't seem to resist. With trigger foods, a small bite just doesn't work. They're the sorts of foods that, when you start eating them, you just can't stop. If you know the food is in the house, you're constantly drawn to it as if it were a magnet. These foods are called trigger foods, because they pull the trigger on over-eating and increase your hunger all day long.

You may not be aware that a certain food is a trigger food for you until you really think about it. Getting in touch with how certain foods make you feel is important. Pay attention to how you feel after you eat something. If a food tastes wonderful, you can't seem to get enough of it, and eating it intensifies your hunger for all foods the rest of the day, then *that* is a trigger food.

Follow these suggestions for dealing with your own trigger foods:

✔ **Exclude all trigger foods from your shopping and house.** If this is too brutal for the rest of the family, include a few of them along with healthier snack choices. Divide the trigger foods into portions and store the portions in the freezer. If you do indulge, it will already be portioned out for you.

✔ **Avoid excess hunger.** It's hard to resist anything when you're hungry, but especially trigger foods. Plan healthy between-meal snacks and never skip a meal.

✔ **Avoid letting stress contribute to overeating.** Maintain your regular meals, exercise, and sleep. Go for a walk before grabbing for the cookie jar.

✔ **Make trigger foods less accessible.** Hide them. Store them in the highest cabinet or in the back of the freezer.

✔ **Develop some great-tasting treats from fruits, sugar-free gelatin, and sugar-free puddings.** Start with recipes in this book and then develop your own.

Feed a craving or ignore it?

A *craving* is an intense and prolonged desire or yearning for a particular food. Most people crave foods high in sugar and fat and low in nutrients. The reasons for the craving are multiple. But, for whatever reason, you can't get the desire for a particular food out of your head and you're afraid it will lead to overeating or bingeing. So, what do you do? Give in to it and risk losing control and going overboard? Or staunchly resist it until it goes away?

If the craving is from simple boredom, you can probably divert your attention away from it. But if it's a true physiological craving, then you probably need to satisfy the craving by eating the food. Most studies indicate that deprivation does not work and may lead to a craving that results in bingeing. If you do give in to the craving, know how to control the amount you eat. Don't bring home a gallon of ice cream, a box of doughnuts, a package of cookies, or an entire pie or cake. Instead go out and buy one scoop of your favorite ice cream, or one doughnut or cookie, or one piece of cake or pie. Eat it slowly, savor each bite, and enjoy it. Then get back on track with your eating plan. One little detour off the eating plan will not upset the progress you've made. It's only when the detours become too frequent that you may be developing a problem.

 If you have a sweet tooth, include a lot of fruit in your diet to satisfy it. Fresh fruit at the peak of ripeness is wonderfully delicious and sweet. If fresh isn't available, try frozen or canned fruits. Mix several kinds together or try frozen bing cherries by themselves for an instant treat. Try topical fruits like mangoes, and unsweetened versions of dried fruits, like raisins and dried pineapple.

Stocking the Fridge

The refrigerator is often the center of the kitchen, which in turn is the center of the home. Try to keep these staples on hand so that you can whip up low-carb meals in minutes:

- ✔ Low-fat or nonfat milk, yogurt, and cheeses (with no more than 5 grams of fat per ounce)

- ✔ Fresh eggs as well as egg-substitutes or egg whites

    ✔ Tub or spray margarines with no trans-fatty acids

    ✔ Low-fat deli meats and turkey bacon

    ✔ Low-fat or nonfat salad dressing

Fruits and veggies are the original fast foods. They're packaged ready to go, and you don't need a knife and fork to eat them.

Keep a variety of fresh fruits and veggies on hand and ready to go. Here are a few ideas to get you started:

    ✔ **Buy apples, pears, or other in-season fruits.** Let kids use the apple wedger to cut them in wedges.

    ✔ **Buy a whole watermelon, keep a bowl of watermelon chunks for an easy snack, or make up several small watermelon wedges to use as a quick side dish to a sandwich or meal.**

    ✔ **Prep your veggies as soon as you get home from the grocery store.** If you buy a head of cauliflower, cucumbers, red peppers, and so on, clean and slice them immediately. Store them in the fridge so that they'll be ready for snacking when you are.

Filling the Freezer

You can buy several items to keep in the freezer to make your low-carb life easier. But make sure you save room to make meals ahead and freeze them, so you'll have healthy low-carb meals ready to go all the time.

Here's the short list of freezer must haves (be sure to check the carb count in the different brands):

    ✔ Low-fat frozen entrees

    ✔ Individual frozen pizzas

    ✔ Frozen unbreaded fish fillets

    ✔ Lean cuts of meat and skinless poultry

    ✔ Light or sugar-free frozen yogurt or ice cream

    ✔ Sugar-free fudge bars or ice cream bars

✔ 100-percent fruit juice concentrates

✔ Frozen vegetables without sauces

Keep some blueberries, seeded cherries, or grapes in the freezer. These are great bite-sized treats and are much better for you than popsicles, frozen novelties, or even juice pops. Choose a diet lemon-lime soda, grapefruit flavored soda, or club soda to pour over a bowl of frozen fruit for a quick, delicious fruit salad.

Organizing the Cupboards and Pantry

Your pantry should have a range of foods, from dried beans and grains to ready-to-go, almost out-of-the-can foods for quick meals. However, that does not mean stocking up on mac and cheese or packaged dinners. You want to choose canned and jarred foods that are still processed as little as possible. Look for canned beans and tomatoes, but skip the spaghetti dinner in a box. You can get roasted red peppers or chilies in a jar, but avoid the urge to get canned soup.

Getting help with already prepped ingredients is fine, but be wary if the only prep you do is heating it in a microwave. If that's the case, the food is likely loaded with preservatives, trans fats, and chemicals your body doesn't need and won't tolerate well over the long haul.

Oils and vinegars

Look for healthy oils, like olive oil, canola oil, and peanut oil or light combination oils. These are better choices than corn oil or any kind of shortening. For details on which oils are healthy, check out Chapter 5.

Nonstick vegetable oil spray is a great addition to any pantry. You can find it in a variety of flavors, including olive oil, garlic, butter, and the like. You can buy oil misters to create your own versions of these. They're available at virtually any store that sells cookware. You can use any kind of oil you have at home. Just make sure that you clean the mister occasionally instead of just refilling it, because the dregs can get rancid if you don't.

Many types of vinegar are available. Vinegars are by nature acidic. Adding an acidic food to a meal lowers the glycemic index (refer to Chapter 2) of the meal. Keep a variety of vinegars on hand to enhance different flavors in salads. Look for different varieties (such as apple cider, balsamic, garlic, raspberry, champagne, cabernet, or zinfandel) to make your own dressings or add a quick no-carb sauce to a meal.

Marinated foods

Marinated vegetables are great as snacks and side dishes. The vinegar they contain helps lower the glycemic index of the foods you eat along with them. Most of these items can be eaten right out of the jar and make great additions to veggie trays or antipastos. Here's a list to start with:

- Sun-dried tomatoes
- Artichoke hearts
- Olives
- Capers
- Marinated vegetables (okra, beans)
- Roasted peppers
- Pickles, pickle relish
- Horseradish, Dijon, spicy, or plain mustard
- Red and white table wine (for cooking)

Canned and jarred foods

Look for these items to help you whip together easy weeknight meals.

- Canned tuna, salmon, or sardines (in water)
- Canned new white potatoes
- Canned vegetables (asparagus, carrots, green beans, mushrooms)

- ✔ Canned fruit packed in light syrup or juice
- ✔ 100-percent fruit preserves
- ✔ Canned chicken or beef bouillon
- ✔ Canned tomatoes and tomato paste
- ✔ Salsa
- ✔ Ketchup
- ✔ Canned or dried beans such as pinto, navy, kidney, limas, garbanzo, peas
- ✔ Fat-free refried beans
- ✔ Natural or low-sugar peanut butter

Grains

These grains are handy additions to your pantry, but remember your portion sizes:

- ✔ Whole-grain pasta, long-grain rice, wild rice
- ✔ Whole-grain flours and cornmeal
- ✔ Oatmeal
- ✔ High-fiber, no sugar, cereals
- ✔ Low-sugar granola or homemade granola

Check out Chapter 5 for the details on how to use your five carb choices each day.

Snacks

These snacks should be used sparingly but can help in a pinch when you need an energy pickup or a sweet-tooth fix:

- ✔ Low-sugar cookies, like vanilla wafers, animal crackers, or gingersnaps
- ✔ Low-fat microwave popcorn
- ✔ Low-carb protein bars, candies, or chips
- ✔ Whole-grain crackers

✔ Sugar-free hot cocoa mix

✔ Sugar-free gelatin and puddings

Seasonings

Variety may be the spice of life, but what would food be without seasoning? Keep these seasonings on hand for quick additions to marinades, sauces, and one-pot meals:

✔ Salt-free seasonings

✔ Garlic and onion, fresh, minced, and powdered

✔ Bouillon cubes or sprinkles

✔ Reduced-sodium soy sauce or Worcestershire sauce

✔ Sugar substitutes

Paying Attention to Safety

Food-borne diseases cause an estimated 76 million illnesses in the United States every year according to the Centers for Disease Control and Prevention. Don't make the mistake of only associating those illnesses with restaurants and public eating places. Even though illnesses occurring in these public places get all the press, food-related illnesses can occur right in your own home.

The cardinal rule of food safety is this: Keep hot foods hot; keep cold foods cold; and keep hands, utensils, and the kitchen clean.

✔ Allow sufficient cooking time for food to reach safe internal temperatures during cooking, and hold the food at a high enough temperature to prevent bacterial growth until it is served. Use a food thermometer to check temperatures.

✔ Go directly home upon leaving the grocery store and immediately unpack foods into the refrigerator or freezer upon your arrival.

✔ Wash the countertops, your hands, and utensils in warm, soapy water before and after each step of food preparation.

Allowing refrigerated foods to warm up to room temperature and allowing cooked foods to cool down to room temperature creates a temperature range conducive to bacteria growth known as the *danger zone*. Between the temperatures of 40 and 140 degrees is the prime growing temperature for bacteria. No food should be kept at that temperature for longer than two hours. The "2-40-140" rule will help you to remember the time and temperature danger zone for foods: No more than 2 hours between 40 degrees F and 140 degrees F.

Here are a few other safety tips that will help keep you and your family safe from food-borne illnesses:

- ✔ **When in doubt, throw it out.** Throw out foods with danger-signaling odors. But be aware that most food poisoning bacteria are odorless, colorless, and tasteless. Do not even *taste* a food that is suspect.

- ✔ **Use separate cutting boards for meat and poultry.** Don't use wooden cutting boards. Bacteria can live in the grooves. Sterilize cutting boards in the dishwasher. Consider buying separate colors for meat and fresh foods like veggies and bread.

- ✔ **Wash and disinfect sponges and towels regularly.** Launder in a bleach solution.

- ✔ **Avoid cross-contamination by washing all surfaces (including your hands) that have been in contact with raw meats, poultry, or eggs.**

- ✔ **Thaw meats or poultry in the refrigerator, not on the kitchen counter.** If you must thaw foods quickly, use cool running water or the microwave.

- ✔ **Do not put cooked food on a plate that was used for raw meat or poultry.** If you bring your raw steaks, chicken, or burgers to the grill on a platter, get a fresh platter for the final product.

- ✔ **Mix foods with utensils, not your hands.** And keep hands and utensils away from your mouth, nose, and hair.

Your refrigerator temperature should be kept at 34 to 40 degrees F. If, in your household, the refrigerator door is opened and closed a lot, keep the temperature near the lower end (34 degrees). Put food in the refrigerator quickly to prevent the growth of bacteria; don't let leftovers sit out for more than two hours (hot dishes for more than an hour). Store foods in plastic bags or covered containers. Keep meat separate from vegetables to prevent cross-contamination.

Keep your freezer at sub-freezing — 0 degrees F. Wrap food in plastic wrap and foil, or store in airtight plastic bags or sealed tubs with the date marked. Place new items in the back, and rotate existing food to the front to help use them in a timely manner. If possible, use leftovers before uncooked meat.

Nonperishable doesn't mean that a food lasts forever; it will perish at some point. Most dry goods now have expiration dates on them. Always follow those dates, when they're available. When they're not available, here are a few guidelines:

- ✔ **Canned foods:** Stored properly, most unopened canned foods keep for at least one year. If the top of a can is bulging, throw it out.

- ✔ **Bottled foods:** Sealed, they last a few months. After they're opened, be sure to refrigerate them. Depending on the food, they can last one week to two months when opened.

- ✔ **Boxes and bags of food:** Sealed, they last for three months to one year; open, they last one week to three months. Store open products in airtight containers to extend their longevity and to prevent odor crossover and insect invasion.

Whole-grain flours and cornmeal may keep best in the freezer. Put the whole package in a large airtight plastic bag before freezing. When baking, take out the portion you need and let it reach room temperature before using.

Chapter 7

Developing a Low-Carb Shopping Strategy

*Y*ou're headed home and you decide to run into the supermarket to pick up milk and bread; you leave 20 minutes later with four bags of groceries. But don't blame yourself. Most supermarkets are laid out in a way that makes dashing in and out difficult to do. From the music that you hear, to the aromas that you smell, you need to be aware of the environment you're entering — so that you can avoid those impulse items that are not part of your healthy eating plan.

In this chapter, I give you the inside scoop on the layout of a supermarket's floor plan. Although I use a supermarket as my example, stores in general have a similar plan.

If it goes in the grocery cart, it goes in the house and ultimately into the mouth. Stop and think before you toss something into your cart.

Knowing Supermarket Layout and Design

In this section, I show you the typical grocery store floor plan, as shown in Figure 7-1.

The most basic and nutritious foods are usually placed in areas around the perimeter of the store. This is where you find milk, bread, meat, and produce. At least one of these staple items is on every shopping list. Locating them around the edge and toward the back of the store provides more opportunity for bright-colored displays to catch your eye.

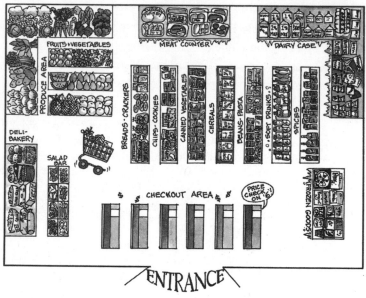

Figure 7-1: The perimeter of the supermarket is your best bet for whole-food choices.

Steering Your Cart toward the Healthy Foods

Put the following locations on your radar screen as targets for healthy food:

✔ **Perimeter:** The healthiest foods are around the perimeter of the store. This is where you'll find the most *whole foods* — foods free from processing and added sugar, salt, and fat.

✔ **Dairy case:** Look for skim, ½%, and 1% milk; low-fat and nonfat yogurt; reduced-fat cheeses; ricotta cheese; and liquid or tub margarines labeled with "no trans fatty acids."

✔ **Produce section:** People study years to memorize all the carotenoids, flavonoids, antioxidants, phytochemicals, and other wonderful stuff in fruits and vegetables. And let's face it, you're probably not that interested in the science behind it all. So just concentrate on filling your cart with color. Get as many colors in there as possible — red, yellow, orange, and especially green — and you'll cover all the bases. Buy fruit in season and in bags. Apples and oranges sold in bags are often cheaper than purchasing the same fruits individually.

Here are a few tips to help you select the best produce.

- Choose produce with a good color, not pale or browning.

- Select firm, not limp or soggy, produce. Hard pieces are not yet ripe; soft pieces are too ripe. If you're making guacamole, select the mushiest avocados you can find — the riper the better.

- Avoid bruised or damaged items.

- Ask the produce manager if you can sample the food before buying. Nothing is more frustrating than getting home and discovering the grapes are sour.

✔ **Meat counter:** Don't fear red meat, but look for the leanest cuts available. Red meat is an important source of zinc and iron. Check out those lean suggestions in Chapter 4.

✔ **Fish market:** Get acquainted with your store's fish market. Fish is a heart-healthy food. The American Heart Association recommends two fish meals a week.

It's best to purchase fresh fish the same day you plan to prepare it. If you don't do that, store fresh fish sandwiched between layers of ice (see Figure 7-2) or in airtight plastic containers. Don't purchase fish with a "fishy" odor.

Figure 7-2: Store fish in layers of ice.

Supermarket salad bars offer a convenient variety of already prepared fruits and vegetables — no cutting, no mess. Also, try prepackaged salads, greens, and slaws. Containers of cut-up fruit (pineapple rings, sliced strawberries, melon balls, kiwi slices, mango, and papaya chunks) can be eaten as is or mixed into cereal or frozen yogurt. You may pay a little more, but sometimes paying for this convenience results in a healthier meal at home than a trip to a fast-food restaurant.

Avoiding Pitfalls in the Aisles

The middle aisles are where all the processed foods are (refer to Figure 7-1). The more ingredients a food has that you can't pronounce, the less it belongs in your shopping cart. But there are some good choices in the aisles if you know where to look.

Here are a few examples of healthy foods that are found in the aisles, rather than at the perimeter of the grocery store:

✔ **Dried beans:** An inexpensive source of protein and fiber, dried beans and peas are a good way to spend one of your carbohydrate choices.

✔ **Peanut butter:** Not all peanut butters are created equal. The healthiest choices are those that contain only peanuts and salt. Some have trace amounts (less than 1 percent) of hydrogenated vegetable oils (trans fatty acids that threaten heart health) or corn syrup. The small amount of hydrogenated oil keeps the peanut butter from separating and makes the peanut butter creamier. Read food labels carefully.

✔ **Whole-grain bread:** Don't assume that breads with names like "whole-grain" are good sources of fiber. You must check the ingredient panel and look for the word *whole*. A *real* whole-grain bread will list "whole-grain wheat flour" as the first or second ingredient. Also, look for brands that contain at least 3 grams of fiber per serving.

✔ **Canned fruits:** Look for fruits canned in a light syrup or in their own juice. They're great to keep in the pantry to add to a meal. Avoid canned fruit juice products that aren't 100-percent juice, and seek out those that have been fortified with vitamin C and calcium. Look for fruit prepackaged in individual serving containers for quick lunchbox additions.

✔ **Canned vegetables:** Canned vegetables are better than no vegetables at all and in some cases may be better. Keep them in the pantry ready to add to a quick meal, salad, or soup.

Recent studies show that the phytochemicals known as *carotenoids* are better absorbed from many cooked, rather than raw, foods. Carotenoids are powerful antioxidants that are present in red, orange, and yellow vegetables and fruits. Lycopene, a phytochemical shown to fight cancer, becomes more available in tomato products that have been exposed to heat, such as canned or stewed tomatoes, pasta sauce, and ketchup. Carrots have higher levels of beta-carotene after cooking. Corn's antioxidant activity is increased the longer it is cooked. However, levels of folate (a B vitamin) and vitamin C can be decreased by cooking.

✔ **Canned soups:** Canned soups are notorious for being high in sodium and fat. Don't assume that just because a soup claims to be low in fat that it's also low in sodium. Look for soups with less than 500 mg of sodium and less than 3 grams of fat per serving.

✔ **Spaghetti sauce:** Like canned soups, spaghetti sauces differ in sodium content and fat content. Look for a sauce with fewer than 500 mg of sodium and 3 grams of fat per serving. Or try making your own spaghetti sauce using unseasoned canned tomato sauce and adding your own minced garlic and fresh basil. You can find brands of tomato sauce with as little as 0 grams of fat and 200 mg of sodium.

✔ **Frozen foods:** Frozen dinners can be a healthy choice if you carefully select them. Look for dinners that contain about 1 cup of vegetables and about 350 to 400 calories. Plan to add a salad, a piece of fruit, or a glass of skim milk to improve the nutritional quality and to make the meal more satisfying. Many frozen dinners are high in sodium and fat so look for dinners with no more than 800 mg of sodium and no more than 30 percent of the daily value for total fat. Keep a few frozen dinners in the freezer. They're perfect for a quick dinner when time is limited or when you just don't feel like cooking.

Frozen vegetables (without sauces) are just as nutritious as fresh. Buy the large-sized bags. Take out what you need and save the rest for later. You can add bags or boxes of frozen veggies to already prepared soups, stews, and casseroles.

Low-carb eating has become so popular that supermarkets often include sections dedicated specifically to low-carb products. Be sure to check out these areas when stocking up on low-carb foods for your pantry.

Deciphering Food Labels

Always read the labels. Get out of the habit of only looking at the fat content. Look at the total carbohydrate content per serving. Determine how much is fiber and how much is sugar. Look at the ingredient list and determine the food sources of the fat, carbohydrate, and fiber. The more dietary fiber in the food the better it is.

What's the skinny on natural peanut butter?

You'll recognize natural peanut butter by the oily layer that forms on the top. Don't pour this oil off. It is a monounsaturated fat and good for your heart. Also, pouring it off will leave a very thick peanut butter that not only sticks to the roof of your mouth but is impossible to spread on bread. You can handle the oil in two ways:

✔ Just turn the jar over until the oil seeps through to the other end.

Periodically rotate the jar to keep the oil evenly dispersed in the peanut butter.

✔ Take a knife and carefully stir the oil back down into the peanut butter. When it's evenly mixed, store the peanut butter in the refrigerator to keep it from separating. When ready to use, take out the portion needed and soften it in the microwave for spreading.

If the food you're evaluating has a high carb count and it's mainly high fructose corn syrup or table sugar, remember that 4 grams of sugar equal 1 teaspoon. Regular 12-ounce cans of soft drink contain 40 grams of carbohydrate — all sugar. That equals 10 teaspoons, or almost ¼ cup. It's a sobering thought.

Check out the serving sizes. All the nutrition information on the label applies to the stated serving size. Don't assume that a small box of any food or beverage is only one serving. Double-check the number of servings per container. Often a 16-ounce bottle contains 2 servings. But who only drinks half a bottle? You may be getting twice the sugar you thought.

Understanding the ingredient panel

Foods listed in the ingredient panel are required to be listed greatest in quantity (by weight) first and then on down the line. A breakfast cereal with sugar listed as first or second on the ingredient panel has more sugar than anything else.

Look for the terms *hydrogenized* or *partially hydrogenated oil* on the ingredient panel. This indicates a source of trans fatty acids. Try to minimize your intake of this fat. You'll find it in many packaged goods, such as cakes, pastries, crackers, cookies, and cereals. For more on trans fats, see Chapter 5.

Fresh produce does not carry a nutrition label. However, the nutrition information should be available. Look for it on a flyer or poster in the produce department. Ask the produce manager if you can't find it.

Discovering the Nutrition Facts label

The Nutrition Facts label issued by the Food and Drug Administration (FDA) in 1994 provides nutrition information relevant to current public health recommendations (see Figure 7-3). Its intent is to show how a food fits into an overall healthy diet. The label carries information that consumers can apply to their individual health needs.

The top section gives you information on the serving size of the food, and how many servings are in the entire container. The middle section of the label gives you details on the nutrients most important to good health. This section helps you to calculate daily limits for fat, cholesterol, sodium, carbohydrate, fiber, and other nutrients. Pay close attention to two things in this section:

- ✔ **Daily Reference Values (DRVs)** are standards for nutrients that have a significant impact on health and disease. DRVs for fat, saturated fat, carbohydrate, fiber, and protein are based on a 2,000-calorie reference diet. The 2,000-calorie level was chosen because it represents a reasonable reference caloric intake for an adult or for children over 4 years of age.

- ✔ **Percent (%) Daily Value:** The % Daily Value shows you how a food fits into your overall diet. If you see that a food contains 200 mg of cholesterol, you may not know if it is high or low in cholesterol. The % Daily Value is the clue. It tells you that one serving of the food has 66 percent of your daily value for cholesterol. A neat trick to use is to remember the 5 and 20 rule: If a food has 5% or less of a nutrient, it is considered low in that nutrient; if it has 20% or more, it's considered high.

Nutrition Facts
Serving Size 1/2 cup (122 g)
Servings Per Container about 3.5

Amount Per Serving

Calories 40	Fat Cal. 5

% Daily Value*

Total Fat 0.5 g	1%
Sodium 5 mg	0%
Total Carb. 9 g	3%
Fiber 5 g	21%
Sugars 4 g	
Protein 2 g	

Vitamin A 300% (80% as beta-carotene)	
Calcium 2%	Iron 4%

Not a significant source of saturated fat, cholesterol, and vitamin C.
*Percent Daily Values are based on a 2,000 calorie diet.

Serving size: This varies from package to package. Serving sizes don't always reflect the typical amount that an adult may eat. In some cases, the serving size may be a very small amount.

Calories: The calories contained in a single serving.

% daily values: The percentage of nutrients that one serving contributes to a 2,000-calorie diet. Parents or children may need more or less than 2,000 calories per day.

Nutrient amounts: The nutritional values of the most important, but not all, vitamins and other nutrients in the product.

Figure 7-3: The Nutrition Facts label.

Prior to the Nutrition Labeling and Education Act, many descriptive terms used on labels were not regulated. Today, food products using descriptive terms on food labels must meet strict regulations.

Nutrient content claims are defined for *one serving*. For example, that means that low-fat cheese has no more than 3 grams of fat per serving.

Considering labels on the Whole Foods Eating Plan

For the Whole Foods Eating Plan, you don't count the carbohydrate in fruits, vegetables, and milk. You only count the carbohydrate in the Yellow Light starchy foods. (See Chapter 5 for the full story.) Fruits, vegetables, and milk will show sugar as part of the total carbohydrate on the food label, but this sugar is the naturally occurring sugar in the food. It is not added sugar.

In the Yellow Light foods, 15 grams of total carbohydrate count as one carbohydrate choice. You may subtract the fiber from the total carbohydrate amount. For example, if one serving of a cereal contains 21 grams of total carbohydrate and 6 grams of dietary fiber, you may subtract the 6 grams of fiber from the total of 21 grams of carbohydrate. This will give you 15 grams of total carbohydrate for one serving, which equals one carb choice.

Many companies that market low-carb foods, such as chips, candies, and breads, include a listing called *net carbs* on their Nutrition Facts labels. These manufacturers have stopped counting the carbs in fiber and artificial sweeteners because they typically have no calories. So, the companies are actually subtracting the carbs they contain from the overall carb count to get the *net carb* count. However, be aware that the carbs in sweeteners such as xylitol, sorbitol, mannitol, and glycerin do contain calories and should be included. Fiber, on the other hand, *can be* subtracted from the total carbohydrates because it has no calories.

The FDA hasn't sanctioned the rather new term "net carb." So, always check the complete list of ingredients, including calories (even in foods labeled low-carb), for an accurate understanding of the nutrition you're getting overall.

Be familiar with all the names in the ingredient list that mean sugar. For the sweet, or not-so-sweet, story on sugar, refer to Chapter 2.

Chapter 8

Smart Choices to Make When Eating Out

. . . .

In This Chapter

▶ Making smart choices in restaurants

▶ Getting to know low-carb-friendly fast-food choices

▶ Planning snacks while traveling

. . . .

*E*ating away from home is so common that it's almost an assumption. A friend of mine says that when she tells her family it's time to eat, they all get in the car! Eating away from home has increased dramatically, and many people feel that you can't possibly eat out and follow a healthy diet at the same time.

Knowing how to find healthy, low-carb options no matter where you eat is crucial. In this chapter, I tell you everything you need to know to do exactly that.

Studying the Menu

Planning ahead makes all the difference when you first begin a new eating regimen, and choosing a low-carb life style is no exception. Create a plan *before* you order, at least until low-carb eating becomes second nature.

If you aren't sure which options to choose on the menu, check out the following tips on great low-carb ordering in a restaurant.

✔ **Appetizers:** Select a smarter appetizer. Start your meals with a bowl of broth-based (not cream-based) soup, salad, fresh fruit, or raw vegetables. Other good choices are tomato juice, clear broth, bouillon, consommé, marinated vegetables, a fresh fruit cup, or steamed fresh seafood.

✔ **Salads:** Almost any salad in a restaurant is better than no salad at all. Look for tossed vegetables, like the traditional lettuce/sliced-tomato/cucumber combo. Or protein-based dishes that include cottage cheese. If you can't be sure that the restaurant serves light or low-calorie dressings, opt for lemon juice or vinegar. And always get it on the side.

✔ **Entrees:** Order roasted, baked, broiled, or grilled poultry, fish, or seafood. Look for lean meats with the fat trimmed. Order your gravy or sauce on the side. Instead of a dinner entree, consider combining a salad with a low-fat appetizer.

✔ **Vegetables:** French fries are not vegetables! They used to be (in their raw form, as potatoes), but once they're peeled and fried, they lose their vegetable status. Look for raw, stewed, steamed, boiled, or stir-fried vegetables. Just about any veggie is a good veggie, until you deep-fry it, so avoid the onion rings, fried mushrooms, and so on.

✔ **Desserts:** Cut back on the sweet stuff. Instead try fresh fruit or fruit juice, fat-free or low-fat yogurt, or gelatin desserts. If you must have a sweet ending to your meal, split the dessert with one or more of your friends. Order one dessert for the table and give everyone a taste.

✔ **Beverages:** Go for black coffee, plain tea, sugar-free soda, or water with lemon. Avoid sugary soft drinks.

Assessing Portion Sizes

Restaurants are known for big portions and enticements to eat more. Recent studies indicate that people eat as much as they're served. If a regular-size burger will satisfy your hunger, but you order the jumbo burger, you'll eat all of the larger burger. You're better off reducing your portion size from the beginning by not ordering the large size.

Splitting Entrees

Splitting an entree with a dining partner is a good way to have a satisfying meal, reduce calories, and save money. But first ask the waiter if the restaurant allows it. Some restaurants allow you to split the entree but will bring doubles of the side items like bread or potatoes. That won't help you. Other restaurants offer half portions of the regular items.

Reducing Liquid Calories

Watch out for beverages. Studies show that people don't adjust their food intake for liquid calories. In other words, people don't eat less just because they're consuming extra calories in sugar-sweetened soft drinks or other beverages. Calories from beverages are purely additive to the diet. In addition to soft drinks, limit alcohol, which adds calories but no nutrition to your meal. Choose plain tea, coffee, or water instead.

Knowing How to Order

Don't be afraid to ask questions about your food. Here are a few tips on the right questions to ask:

- If you don't know what's in a dish or don't know the serving size, ask.
- Ask for the chips or bread to be brought with the meal, or not at all.
- Ask for a fruit cup as an appetizer or the breakfast melon for dessert.
- Confirm that you can order foods that are not breaded or fried. If the food comes breaded, peel off the breading.
- Ask for substitutions. If you can't get a substitute, just ask that the high-fat carb food be left off your plate.
- Ask for low-calorie items, such as salad dressing, even if they're not on the menu.
- Ask for fish or meat broiled with no extra butter.
- Ask for sauces, gravy, and salad dressings on the side.

Making Sensible Fast-food Selections

The average American eats in a fast-food restaurant four times a week. If you're having fast food for one meal, let your other meals that day contain healthier foods like fruits and vegetables.

✔ **Pizza restaurants:** Pizza can be a good fast-food choice. Go for thin-crust pizza with vegetable toppings. Limit yourself to one or two slices or a personal-pan pizza. If you plan for leftovers, put them away and out of sight before you dig in.

✔ **Burger joints:** Probably the most-common fast-food experience is the ever-present burger restaurant. The hamburger is the quintessential American food. Here's how you can continue to indulge, the low-carb way:

  • Junior-size cheeseburger

  • Kid-size or small French fries

  • Side salad with low-fat dressing

  • Orange juice or diet soft drink

✔ **Buffet-style restaurants:** If you end up at a buffet table, try this trick: Picture your plate and mentally divide it into quarters. Select fruit, vegetables, and lean proteins for three-fourths of the plate. The last quarter is reserved for any starchy carbs or sweet items.

Evaluating Carry-out Options

Many take-out counters in specialty food stores and super-markets offer lightly stir-fried or roasted vegetables. This healthy indulgence costs about the same price as a high-calorie dessert. Look for fresh fruit whole or cut up. Alternately, keep fruit handy with you at all times — at home, on your desk, in your car. That way, even if the restaurant doesn't offer it, you don't have to go without.

Carry bottled water, diet colas, or fruit juice in your cooler rather than sugary soft drinks. Pack fresh fruit for snacking. Fresh fruit is offered at most sandwich shops, airports, mall food courts, and outdoor refreshment stands. Pack snacks when you travel, though, just in case you can't find a healthy snack.

Eating smart while you're traveling can really help minimize the adverse affects of the stress that usually goes along with it. And just because you're on the go, it's not time to forget all your rules of healthy eating.

✔ **Practice portion control.**

✔ **Eat slowly.**

✔ **Reduce stress by walking or stretching.**

✔ **Keep a food log and evaluate your choices against the Whole Foods Eating Plan.**

✔ **Be wary of impulse eating.**

✔ **Avoid skipping meals.**

✔ **Eat preventively (healthy snacking) to take the edge off your appetite.**

✔ **If your food choices were less than ideal, then compensate by choosing healthier foods at your other meals.** Healthy eating is not made up of one food or one meal. It's your overall food intake that counts.

✔ **Exercise to work off your extra food intake.**

Seeing How Your Favorite Ethnic Foods Stack Up

One major reason people choose to eat out (after convenience of course) is to get a different variety of foods than they prepare for themselves at home. Most ethnic restaurants have plenty of healthy choices, however.

✔ **Chinese:** Authentic Chinese food features plenty of vegetables and lean meat, but watch out for deep-fried meats in sugary sauces like the one on the ever-popular General Tsao's chicken or sweet-and-sour pork. Limit your intake of the starchy, Asian-style sticky white rice. Opt for oriental noodles, like lo mein instead. Try to avoid the deep-fried foods, like egg rolls; the sweet sauces can have a lot of sugar.

✔ **Italian:** Pasta dishes and bread can quickly exceed your carb limit. Thin-crust pizza with vegetable toppings is a good choice. Look for antipasto for a great selection of meats, cheeses, and marinated vegetables. Try seafood and meat dishes. All are great with a big salad. Skip anything parmigiana-style unless you confirm that the cutlets aren't breaded.

✔ **Mexican:** Most Mexican restaurants in the United States serve high-starch, high-fat foods like refried beans, rice, enchiladas, and tortillas. A basket of chips and salsa, which are denser in calories than they are in nutrients are certainly a setup for disaster. Try sticking with grilled seafood and chicken dishes, black beans, and entrees such as fajitas. Ask the waiter to bring the chips *with* the meal instead of before. It only takes a big handful of chips to equal a carbohydrate choice.

Index

Ten Benefits of Low-Carb Eating

Improved Glucose Control

One of the first benefits of reducing the total amount of carbohydrate (especially the refined carbohydrate foods) in your diet is usually an improvement in your blood glucose (blood sugar) level. Let the carbohydrate foods that you do choose to eat be fruits, vegetables, and whole-grain or unrefined grain foods. You'll notice fewer sugar highs and sugar lows, which create hunger.

Better Appetite Control

You'll have a normal hunger at mealtimes, but it will be easily satisfied by the foods on the Whole Foods Eating Plan. You'll no longer have periods of ravenous hunger. On those days when you *are* hungrier, you have a variety of Green Light foods to satisfy that hunger and still maintain your healthy eating plan.

Improved Concentration

As your blood sugar becomes more stable, you'll notice that you can concentrate better. You'll no longer feel lethargic and barely able to hold your eyes open after lunch.

Weight Maintenance

On the Whole Foods Eating Plan, you'll notice that you feel more comfortable in your clothes and your body feels lighter. Your weight won't increase; in fact, you'll probably lose a few pounds.

Improved Blood Pressure

The Whole Foods Eating Plan provides low-fat dairy products, protein, calcium, potassium, magnesium, and fiber — all nutrients proven to lower your blood pressure. The Whole Foods Eating Plan allows you to rid yourself of extra water you may be retaining. This loss of excess water not only makes you feel better, it helps to lower your blood pressure.

Improved Cholesterol

The Whole Foods Eating Plan significantly lowers your intake of saturated fat and trans fatty acids as well as lowers your overall carbohydrate intake. You're encouraged to choose monounsaturated fats and to increase your intake of fish supplying omega-3 fatty acids. These dietary changes are important in lowering your total cholesterol, LDL cholesterol, and triglyceride levels in your blood.

Improved Sleep

Lowering the amount of carbohydrate and the amount of food that you eat in the evening will allow you to sleep better. Your body is able to fully relax because it isn't up digesting a heavy meal. Stabilizing your blood sugar and getting rid of excess water cuts down on your number of trips to the bathroom. You'll be able to sleep longer without being disturbed. You'll feel rested when you awaken in the morning because you had a good night's sleep.

More Energy

You'll definitely notice that you have a lot more energy.

Better Mood

When you just feel better all over, your mood improves. You're happier and you respond to people with a more positive attitude. You feel stronger, better-rested, and healthy.

More Self-Confidence

Everything comes together with a more confident you. Your health improves, your appetite is controlled, your concentration is better, your weight is better controlled, you sleep better, you get more done, and you're happier and more confident.

Low-Carb Tips For Dummies

How to Eat Smarter

- Build your meals around fruits, vegetables, and lean protein food sources.
- Choose whole grains or legumes for your daily carb choices. Minimize your intake of processed foods.
- Choose very-low-fat milk and dairy foods.
- Choose monounsaturated rather than saturated fats.
- Eat three or four meals per day. Never starve yourself or skip meals. If you eat between meals, eat Green Light foods, such as apples or oranges, for a healthy snack.
- Do not eat a full meal right before bedtime. A bedtime snack such as nonfat yogurt or cottage cheese and fruit is okay.
- Drink plenty of water — eight glasses a day.
- Exercise moderately 30 to 60 minutes at least five times a week.
- Practice the 90-percent/10-percent rule: Follow this low-carb eating 90 percent of the time, and treat yourself to a favorite food 10 percent of the time.

How to Stick with the Plan

- **Set up your kitchen for success.** Always have low-carb-friendly foods on hand ready to eat. Remove as many irresistible temptations as possible.
- **Avoid excessive hunger.** Eat before you're starving. When you're ravenous, it's tougher to make a healthy choice.
- **Prepare snacks in grab-and-go sizes.** Make prepackaged snacks from cut-up veggies and whole wheat crackers in resealable plastic bags. Fresh fruit is already prepackaged for your convenience so carry some wherever you go.
- **Eat a variety of foods** for better nutrition.
- **Find activities and exercises that you enjoy.** If you find something you really enjoy, you're more apt to do it every day. If you're social, find friends to walk with. If you look forward to exercise as your "alone time," plan times when you can work out alone. Make your workout personal.
- **Forgive yourself when you fail.** Everyone experiences a setback from time to time. Figure out where you went wrong and get going again!

Green-Light Snack List

Here's a quick list of snacks to keep you going. Enjoy these snacks anytime, as often as you like.

- A juicy orange
- A bunch of grapes
- An 8-ounce container of low-fat yogurt
- A can of unsweetened applesauce, diced peaches, or mixed fruit
- A glass of skim, ½%, or 1% milk
- Dried apricots
- A handful of raisins
- A big green or red apple
- Raw vegetables with low-fat salad dressing
- Sliced turkey rolled up in a lettuce leaf
- Boiled shrimp with zesty cocktail sauce
- Skim-milk mozzarella string cheese

Must-Haves for the Low-Carb Pantry

- Canned or bottled foods:
  - Canned tuna, salmon, or sardines (in water)
  - Canned vegetables (asparagus, carrots, green beans, mushrooms, and so on)
  - Canned fruit packed in light syrup or juice
  - 100-percent-fruit preserves
  - Canned chicken or beef bouillon
  - Canned tomatoes and tomato paste
  - Salsa
  - Ketchup
  - Canned or dried beans such as pinto, navy, kidney, lima, garbanzo, peas
  - Fat-free refried beans
  - Natural or low-sugar peanut butter
  - Sun-dried tomatoes
  - Artichoke hearts
  - Olives
  - Capers
  - Marinated vegetables (okra, beans)
  - Roasted peppers
  - Pickles and pickle relish
  - Horseradish, Dijon, spicy, or plain mustard
  - Red and white table wine (for cooking)
- Grains:
  - Whole-grain pasta, long-grain rice, wild rice
  - Whole-grain flours and cornmeal
  - Oatmeal
  - High-fiber, no-sugar cereals
  - Low-sugar granola or homemade granola
  - Quinoa
  - Roasted soynuts
- Seasonings:
  - Salt-free seasonings
  - Garlic and onion, minced and powder
  - Bouillon cubes or sprinkles
  - Reduced-sodium soy sauce or Worcestershire sauce
  - Sugar substitutes
- Oils and vinegars:
  - Nonstick vegetable oil spray
  - Healthy oils (olive oil, canola oil, peanut oil, or light combination oils)